Kathy Galloway is the Leader of the Iona Community, and lives in Glasgow. She is a practical theologian, campaigner and writer. The major focus of her work has always been with social justice issues, especially relating to people living in poverty and to women. She was formerly employed by Church Action on Poverty with a special remit to develop participatory approaches to overcoming poverty with those who experience it. She is the author of nine books of theology, liturgy and poetry, including *A Story to Live By* (London: SPCK, 1999), *Walking in Darkness and Light: Sermons and Reflections* (Edinburgh: St Andrew Press, 2001) and *The Dream of Learning Our True Name* (Glasgow: Wild Goose Publications, 2004). She is a patron of the Student Christian Movement, has travelled widely and has acted as a consultant for, among others, the World Council of Churches, the Lambeth Conference and the World Alliance of Reformed Churches.

D0309794

SHARING THE BLESSING

Overcoming Poverty and Working for Justice

KATHY GALLOWAY

First published in Great Britain in 2008 by

Society for Promoting Christian Knowledge
36 Causton Street
London SW1P 4ST

and

Christian Aid
35 Lower Marsh
London SE1 7RL

British Library Cataloguing-in-Publication Data
A catalogue record for this book is available from the British Library

ISBN 978–0–281–05949–2

3 5 7 9 10 8 6 4 2

Typeset by Graphicraft Ltd, Hong Kong
Printed in Great Britain by Ashford Colour Press

Produced on paper from sustainable forests

Contents

Acknowledgements

Part of Chapter 1 was first given as the John Wheatley Memorial Lecture 2003 and published by the Christian Socialist Movement, <www.thecsm.org.uk>.

Part of Chapter 5 was first published in *Die Macht der Wurde: Globalisierung neu denken* (Gütersloh: Gütersloher Verlagshaus, 2007).

I am grateful to Niall Cooper, Peter Cruchley-Jones, Peter Millar, Lesley Orr and Eurig Scandrett for their ideas and collegiality and for the inspiration of the Accra Confession, *Covenanting for Justice in the Economy and the Earth*, of the World Alliance of Reformed Churches.

I am also grateful to the following for permission to quote from their work: Janet Morley, John L. Bell, Nathan Segal, Naomi Littlebear Morena and Tafelberg Publishers for Edwin Cameron, *Witness to AIDS*. Copyright acknowledgements can be found in the Notes section at the back of the book.

My thanks to Kate Tuckett, Rebecca Mulhearn, Hannah Ward, Rima Devereaux and the rest of the patient and helpful editorial and production staff of Christian Aid and SPCK.

Introduction: Born into complicity

For more than sixty years, Christian Aid has been one of the strongest prophetic voices in Britain, not only working across the world in relieving poverty but also addressing the causes of that poverty. Prophetic voices are those which read the signs of the times in the light of the justice and love of God, and speak out against all which distorts or diminishes the image of God in human beings. In doing so, they may come into conflict with the status quo, with powerful interests which have an investment in the way things are. They may struggle with questions of resisting and confronting established power.

The majority of people alive in the world today find themselves at the sharp end of the dominant power that is our economic system. In the global economic landscape, there are whole communities, even countries, which are almost entirely redundant to the global economy. They have no capital. Their labour is either unwanted or low-waged. They have very little consumer clout because they don't have enough spending power to be attractive except to moneylenders, drug dealers and arms traders.

This scenario is one which relentlessly distorts or diminishes the image of God in human beings. It is also one in which people come into conflict with the status quo, with powerful interests which have an investment in the way things are. They too may struggle with questions of resisting and confronting established power. This is an overbearing power, acutest of course in the poorest countries of the world, but equally present in pervasive ways in western countries. But as people of faith, we believe that in the face of the poorest, most powerless, most insignificant person, we see the image of God. And we believe, with Jacob, with Moses, with Peter and James and John on the mountain with Jesus, that when we see the face of God, the place whereon we stand is holy ground.

So we are also called, as people of faith, to be prophetic voices, reading the signs of the times in the light of the justice and love of God, and speaking out against all which distorts or diminishes the image of God in human beings. This is both a spiritual and a political calling. Millions of people across the world have responded to this calling in a global justice movement. Their campaigning takes many forms – on trade justice, debt cancellation, environmental activism, human rights and peacemaking. But these things require more than just a political and economic response. They require a spiritual one too.

As Christians oriented towards Jesus, hungering and thirsting for justice, for right relationships, we try to follow him through discernment, directed and challenged and inspired through the ways we pray, sing, share word and sacrament, keep silence, laugh, weep, struggle and hope. So, we trust, we may be guided to appropriate and just public witness, community action, political lobbying, creating the alternative local economics which challenge powerful hegemonies, and standing in solidarity with those who are treated unjustly.

The judgement of Micah

The reality of judgement is a note that resonates through the book of Micah. One of the things that gives the great prophetic voices of the Hebrew Bible (what Christians commonly call the Old Testament) such power is that they speak from and to all sections of society. But Micah, perhaps more than any of the others, speaks with the voice of the poor. This peasant farmer, with the suspicion of the countryman for a so-called progress which will leave the poor even poorer, calls the people of Israel to account for their crimes; and he is quite clear about what these are:

- the oppression of the weak by the strong;
- the expropriation of peasants from their land;
- the eviction of smallholders;
- the enslavement of children.

Now we know very well that nearly three thousand years later, none of these crimes has disappeared from the face of the earth, and we rightly stand in judgement against them, and may be actively involved in campaigning against them. By the authority of scripture, with the authorization of church and tradition, we read the prophetic texts against a world which practises such things, and the world is found wanting.

But it is also important to remember that the words of the prophets were addressed quite specifically to the community of faith, to the people of the covenant. The Hebrew prophets did not appear out of nowhere, their critique was not an external one; they stood within a prophetic tradition and it was because of their belonging within the community that they understood so well the nature of the faith of Israel. Their critique was historical, contextual, directed against specific concrete social and economic practices in a particular place at a particular time. In the words of George MacLeod, founder of the Iona Community, they were not prepared to tolerate 'the obscenity of the now'.

Although their interventions were political in nature, and had direct (and often for them unpleasant) political consequences, their motivation lay elsewhere. It was rooted in a passionate belief that the covenant relationship of God with Israel demanded that the relationships of the people with each other should reflect and replicate that covenant. It was precisely because they were people who had been liberated by the Exodus and had received both the Law and the promise that the community of faith was particularly under judgement. Of all people, they were the ones who should turn from oppressing and enslaving others. Through the voice of Micah, the religiously pious, those who were attached to their own pure identity as the chosen people, were being judged by the poor of the particular world of that little part of the Ancient Near East.

And as followers of Jesus, sharers in the new covenant, we too must take a relationship to the judgement of the world. By the authority of scripture, church and tradition, we stand in judgement on the world and find it wanting. But that judgement is a two-edged sword.

The first time I travelled outside the West, more than twenty years ago to an international peace conference organized by the Christian Conference of Asia, my well-meaning, white, western liberal map of the world was shredded into tiny pieces. The experience shattered my illusions, my confidence and all but shattered my faith, as I knew myself for the first time, not just in theory but in reality, as part of an oppressive, dehumanizing, environmentally disastrous world order. So many conflicts and injustices had British imperialism in there somewhere. Our considerable involvement in the global arms trade made it possible for many countries to make war. But war is not only waged with weapons. War is waged by economic policy, by market forces, by trade rules, by property rights of every kind, from land to intellectual. And it is waged by environmental choices and business interests, as uprooted, dispossessed and threatened people everywhere from Bangladesh to Brazil can tell us. We are always, somewhere in the world, complicit.

I became voiceless. I had nothing to say that could adequately express my shame. Silence seemed the only appropriate response. I had come face to face with the complicity with evil into which I had been born; what the church has classically called, in a somewhat misunderstood phrase, original sin.

This experience of judgement was for me the equivalent of hearing the voice of Micah. It was hearing all my texts, all my scripts, all my maps being read from another perspective. As a woman in the Christian church, I had some experience of what it is like to read from the margins; which has historically been to be overlooked, dismissed, talked down to and talked down, sometimes to be all but invisible. But it is a lifelong journey to hear the judgement that says: God is only colour-blind if you are white; it may be easier to be ecumenical in Scotland if you are Protestant; liberal democracy has a different ring to it if you're a sub-Saharan African country bleeding dry to meet your debt repayments to the IMF; hating the sin but loving the sinner may be a more loaded message if you're gay than if you're straight.

It took me many months to see that, though I had been born into complicity, I was not responsible for what I did not do. I had no choice about the complicity I had been born into – but I was responsible for the complicity I *did* have a choice about. I could say, 'This is the way things are – but I beg to differ.' I could be a non-conformist. I could choose in every way open to me to put an end to complicity.

Hope is a hot love story

My activism has been shaped by the Iona Community, which began in 1938, just before the outbreak of the Second World War. In a catastrophically unjust and violent world, a key question for us is one which Martin Luther King asked, 'How do we keep on keeping on?' Or, to put it another way, 'What is our spirituality for the long haul?' How do we keep hope alive? For me, hope began with the refusal of complicity, with becoming a non-conformist, a dissenter. My Asian experience was profoundly important, because it took me from shame and conviction of sin through repentance to conversion. It took me from what was in reality a kind of youthful, western, liberal optimism rooted in the myth of progress to a different kind of hope.

It is of the essence of Christianity that it is historical; it does not apply to some abstract or spiritual realm outside the temporal. Reality does not allow us to escape from history – we live with the consequences of the past at every moment – and neither does the gospel. We are required, as a fact of our liberation, to engage with history.

Neither is the hope in which we live simply a matter of being forward-looking, of seeing humanity as progressing steadily on to a better future. That was the Enlightenment model, and as much as we progressed, and we did, we also regressed horrendously in the twentieth century. Nevertheless, though we carry our history with us, we do carry it into a different future. The theologian Kosuke Koyama writes:

> Is hope related to the future? Yes. But even more, it is related to love. Hope is not a time-story. It is a love-story. The gospel dares to place love above time. All the healing stories of the gospels, and ultimately the confession of the faith that 'on the third day he rose again from the dead' point to this awesome truth. Hope is as impassioned by love as is every healing word and action of Jesus . . . hope is a hot love story. What gives hope is not time, but the power of love.[1]

This different way of thinking about hope, while remaining absolutely grounded in the historical process, removes it from captivity to time. Hope, in this deep and powerful meaning, exists in time, but is not limited by it. Hope is the refusal of complicity. Hope is to work for something because it is good. Hope is a hot love story. All of this is a way of saying that I do not think that hope is a feeling. Hope is a choice and then it is an action. It is inevitable that western people committed to justice activism should sometimes feel despairing in the face of our own knowledge of complicity, and this is particularly the case when all our efforts seem to be met with governmental intransigence or indifference. But this is not a time to lose our nerve. To feel hopeful is a luxury mostly only enjoyed by people who live in stable, peaceful democracies who have the option to feel despairing. To *live hopefully* is a daily decision made by people who have nothing else to retreat to. One of the things that has always amazed me in my travelling is the capacity to live hopefully to be found in people whose lives are precarious, threatened, filled with unjust and unwarranted suffering, to say 'Yes' to the gift of life with far greater humility, generosity and joy than I ever do.

To work for global justice requires patience and persistence. Structural change is slow and difficult and costly. This book is about how to be part of that change. It has been written with a number of objectives:

- to offer a reflection on the spirituality and practice of working for justice and towards overcoming local and global poverty;
- to offer spiritual and practical resources for resistance and persistence in this work;
- to encourage people to think spiritually and creatively around issues of economics, globalization, migration, etc., which are often difficult for us to link with our faith;
- to put a human face on huge social issues that can so easily seem abstract and distant;
- to engage constructively with the compromises, disappointments and failures of engaging in this work from a position of privilege and empowerment, so that, while realistic about the injustices those in the rich world profit by, we are not paralysed by guilt or defensiveness, which are of no use to anyone;
- to affirm the truth that it is in sharing the suffering of other parts of the body that we also share their joy.

I hope it meets at least some of these objectives.

> Oh God,
> you have made us for yourself,
> and against your longing there is no defence.

Mark us with your love,
and release in us a passion for your justice
in our disfigured world;
that we may turn from our guilt and face you,
our heart's desire.[2]

1

The spirituality of economics

I am not an economist, I am a practical theologian. But I am a theologian whose practice has involved a lifelong engagement with people living in poverty, and therefore with economics. And increasingly I have become interested in the spirituality of economics. Now these are two words which are not often found together. A friend once said to me, 'I see you are writing on the economics of spirituality,' and it may very well be that that is what I am doing. But I think they are actually inseparable if we are truly to understand either of them. Spirituality is a word which is understood in a multiplicity of ways, so in the interest of precision, I will give you *my* definition of it, which will form the basis of what I write. You may not agree with this definition, but hopefully you'll know what I'm talking about. It is indebted to the Latin American theologian, Jon Sobrino.

Once, Jesus was talking to the Pharisees about spirituality (or was it economics?) and he used the analogy of a cup, saying, 'Did not God, who made the outside, also make the inside?' (Luke 11.40). Our spirituality is our profoundest motivation, those instincts, intuitions, longings and desires that move us, animate us, inspire us. These words all have their origins in words for breathing. It is the force that moves us from behind or below or before. But it is also our ultimate concern or orientation or goal, that person, ideal or value that attracts us, that draws us, towards which we go. If you like, our spirituality is the inside of the cup.

But our spirituality is not just interiority. It is also our choices and actions; it is where spirit is given flesh, where intention becomes action, where we practise what we preach. Our spirituality shows up just as much in how we spend our money, our time and our abilities, as in how we say our prayers. If you like, it's how we use the cup.

And our spirituality is also our relationships: with our environment, with other people, with our own most hidden and unknown selves. If you like, it's who we share the cup with.

Everyone has a spirituality, just as everyone has a physicality. Some spiritualities show up dressed in strange clothes. A fervent football fan might be most profoundly motivated by loyalty to his team; his ultimate concern might be that they should win the European Cup; all his choices and actions would be directed to enabling him to follow and support the team and his relationships would all be lived in the light of, and affected by, for good or bad, his passion. But there would be many familiar features in his spirituality: loyalty, devotion and hope would all be there. Of course, other spiritualities – such as that of Nazism, for example – are profoundly perverse and distorted.

We pay much attention to our physicality but often less to the care and nurture of our spirituality. We want to be whole people, or, we might say, we want to become our true selves, to be fully alive, to realize our potential. But the gap between our longings and aspirations and the way we actually live can be hugely painful and damaging, especially if our spirituality is unnamed, unrecognized and unloved. So we need the help, insight and support of others to integrate our intentions and our actions. Spiritualities are not just individual, they are collective. Communities of many kinds also have a spirituality. But can systems have a spirituality?

The global economy

In the years immediately after the Second World War, many countries of the global South began a long process of decolonization, often accompanied by great conflict and violence, as happened, for example, in India, Algeria and Kenya. Sometimes this conflict was caused by the reluctance of the colonial power to cede sovereignty, influence and a ready source of raw materials. Sometimes it was the result of ethnic or tribal dispute; these were often brought about or exacerbated by somewhat arbitrary borders and boundaries drawn by the colonial powers, which took little account of local and precolonial ethnicities and loyalties. Sometimes it happened because the colonial powers had become permanent settlers and, considering that the country belonged to them, they wished to remain the dominant force, as in South Africa and Algeria.

Nevertheless, it seemed as if a new era was dawning for these countries. They would also develop and take their rightful places in the modern world. Many western churches, aid agencies and mission partners were eager to support these countries, not only with funding but with technical, educational and medical help and training. By the 1960s, the gap between the rich countries and the poor countries was smaller than ever before. But the early 1970s saw the gap open up again when poor countries began to be caught in a trap of spiralling debt.

Much of this debt was amassed following the 1973 oil crisis when the western members of OPEC (the Organization of the Petroleum Exporting Countries) pushed the price of oil up, thus making a number of oil-producing countries in the Middle East extremely wealthy. They deposited most of this money in large western banks. Awash with capital, these banks were eager to lend money to developing countries without much attention to where the money would be spent or whether countries would be capable of repaying the amount. While some of this money went towards trying to improve the living standards for those in the countries, most of the loans never reached the poor of the country, either going towards large-scale development projects, some of which proved of little value, or to the private bank accounts of dictators. Overall, about one-fifth of loans went to arms.

Rising interest rates on borrowing created a situation where poor countries became increasingly unable to meet their loan repayments. Many found themselves in a situation where the interest on the debt exceeded the amount that the country produced, thus preventing the debt ever being paid back. Though countries were still paying huge amounts of money (and have usually mostly repaid the original loan several times over), the interest went on growing to the point where it became clear that it was *unpayable*. The more they were unable to pay back, the bigger the debt became. It was as if a mortgage just went on getting bigger and bigger, no matter how many times one repaid the cost of the house. This kind of debt could be considered a method of oppression or control of poor countries by rich countries; a form of debt slavery at the level of nations caused by irresponsible and immoral lending on a global scale.

Faced with the possibility of losing their investments, lenders, mostly through what were known as the Bretton Woods Institutions (organizations set up after the war to assist poor countries, primarily the World Bank and the International Monetary Fund) proposed what were called structural adjustment programmes to fundamentally reorient southern economies. Most called for the drastic reduction in public welfare spending, focusing economic output on direct export and resource extraction, providing an attractive investment climate to multinational investors, increasing the fluidity of investment flows (by replacing foreign direct investment with the opening of stock markets) and generally enhancing the rights of foreign investors vis-à-vis national laws. This became the dominant economic model for much of the world's population.

Combined with unfair, western-biased protectionism and terms of trade, poor countries were unable to decide and manage their own economies, lost power and face at home, and saw the post-war advances in health, education, infrastructure and overcoming poverty rolled back alarmingly. These countries were devastated. It was a form of neocolonialism; no longer able to control poor countries through military and political power, the West could now do it through economic power. Much of the hostility to the West evidenced in other parts of the world stems from the humiliations and privations brought about by the debt crisis and structural adjustment, which all worked considerably to the benefit of rich countries.

In Britain, people began to be familiar with media images of starving children, squalid slums and rampant disease. This had a number of effects. One was the tendency for many in the West to see global poverty as the result of southern fecklessness, ignorance, overpopulation, war – in effect, as 'their fault'. Many felt that 'charity begins at home', without taking on board the complex causes of poverty, and the role of the West in helping to impoverish the so-called 'third world'. In this context, it was hard to make the links between poverty in Britain and poverty in the world's poorest countries visible.

The second difficulty lay in addressing the recognized and well-documented failures of the predominant development models since the Second World War. Because so many development initiatives and projects, especially under structural adjustment, were too exclusively based on western ideas of progress, economics, social life and values, technology and so on, many of them damaged the communities they sought to support, uprooted and weakened them, and alienated them from their own cultural and spiritual roots and resources. People were being excluded, not just from setting the goals of their development, but from shaping its means. This sense of powerlessness is also found in the West, especially among those whom society often designates as 'losers' or 'the underclass'.

In the years since then, none of this has got any better. In the midst of a hugely accelerated pace of change, we are confronting in equal measure unparalleled opportunities and unparalleled threats. Significant parts of the human population, particularly in the West, are healthier, wealthier and enjoy greater opportunities for self-realization than ever before. At the same time, the gap between rich and poor is growing, huge parts of humanity live on the margins of destitution, uprooted peoples number tens of millions and wars and pandemics devastate dozens of countries. The fabric and future of life itself – water, air, the human genome – is facing increasing commodification. On one hand the wealth of consumer nations and on the other the poverty of energy-poor countries have caused an ecological holocaust which threatens the continuation of the planet. In the last 25 years alone, we have destroyed one-third of the world's renewable resources.[1]

The globalization of markets has proved an unstoppable colossus, kicking its way through well-intentioned but ineffectual legislation designed to protect the environment, workforces and local communities. American citizens have been as unable to resist the rolling back of such legislation as Indian, Brazilian or Malaysian citizens. Such powerlessness is not confined to people living in poverty globally; it affects our own legislators equally. A few years ago, the Scottish Executive produced a Social Justice Strategy; it attempted to address poverty in Scotland under a number of headings, setting targets and outlining milestones by which to measure progress along the way. There is no reason to doubt the good faith of those attempting to implement this strategy, nor would I wish to deny its many achievements. But like the government at UK level, it had to engage with the fact that, despite their best efforts, the gap between rich and poor in Scotland continues to grow, and that there is a level of entrenched or intransigent poverty in Britain that all their efforts are unable to shift.

Stakeholding in the global economy

In the global economic landscape, there are a number of ways of being a stakeholder, which offer a different size of stake, and of power. You can be someone with *capital*, that is, individual accumulated wealth owned by you at a given moment, as distinct from income such as a salary, wage or benefit received during a certain period. Your capital might be land, property, money, stocks and shares, gold, works of art; if you have a house, it will be the equity, that is, any profit you might make in reselling it, after you've paid off your original loan plus the interest. The economic value of any of these assets is not fixed, and you do not determine their value. Their value is determined by market forces.

Markets determine value by a number of criteria. For example, the value of a house will depend on such things as its spaciousness, its condition, its convenience, its stylishness, its location and its scarcity. Broadly speaking, property values are based on beauty, craftsmanship, and the ability to maximize the space between human beings while minimizing their distance from services and utilities – much the same values as pertain with cars, air travel, and indeed with health and education when these are privately purchased. You may love your small flat in an inner-city area, it may have huge cultural and spiritual value for you, but that will not show up in its selling price.

There are some particularly talented people whose brains or bodies are considered so desirable in market terms that they in themselves *are* their own capital; their value is far more than they earn; a David Beckham, for example, or a J. K. Rowling. But that value only applies as long as they are in possession of the qualities that make them attractive to the market – their talent, its rarity, its worth to football or the world's reading children. It's unlikely Beckham will have the same value in thirty years. *In the market, value is always extrinsic.* Nothing has value in and for itself, only for what it can be sold for.

Or you can be a stakeholder in the economic landscape through your *labour*, the work of your brain or hands, by your skill, experience or muscle. Again, your labour is only worth what the market determines. If you're a brain surgeon or a member of a chart-topping band you're worth quite a lot, because your skills are rare and in demand, or because a great many people want to buy your records. If you're a firefighter or a nurse, you're worth a bit less, because you're not so rare – but you still have a reasonable stake. If you're a cleaner or an out-worker in the clothing industry, your value is very low, because anyone can do what you're doing, so it's easy to replace you. You're worth the minimum wage, or less. But what if no one wants you in the labour market, perhaps because you're too old, or unskilled or inarticulate or unattractive? What if you are someone like the woman who said to me once after dozens of unsuccessful job applications, 'It feels like there are too many people in the world, and I'm one'? Then your value is set at the level of income support. And that's a problem, because then you are excluded from the only other way of having an eco-nomic stake, which is as a consumer.

In the economic landscape of Britain, there are whole com-munities which are almost entirely redundant to the economy. They have little market value. Their society does not value them, to the point where their children may be suffering from malnutrition. Furthermore, these communities are most likely to be the ones which are considered socially undesirable and politically irrelevant. That is, they are a blot on the landscape, and most of them don't vote, or their votes are taken for granted.

I said almost entirely redundant to the economy. But not quite. There is one group of traders to whom such commun-ities are the most profitable of all. They are the people who sell money. Or, to give them their old name, moneylenders. It's not just in Africa that indebtedness is both a major consequence and a major cause of poverty. Scotland is now the most heavily indebted country in Europe, and in Britain we are indebted to 125 per cent of household income. Of course, borrowing money is part and parcel of economic life across the globe; it's not new, and it's not confined to the poor. The world's big-gest debtor by a long way is the United States government. Consumer credit is what's driving western economies. No, what's really interesting in looking at the economic landscape is not that people borrow money. It's that the people who have the least pay the most to do so. It's a microcosm of the whole world!

Poor people have to borrow money to counteract the consequences of being redundant to the economy. There is increasing evidence that people get into unsustainable debt because they simply do not have enough money to pay for basic necessities, never mind the things that most of us in Britain take for granted as a measure of social inclusion (warm clothing, a holiday, school activities for children). Furthermore, because people living in poverty are denied access to the normal and more affordable sources of credit, such as bank accounts, many are pushed towards legal and illegal moneylenders. Even the legal interest rates, charged on small loans of, say, £200 may be as much as 160 per cent APR, thus deepening the cycle of indebtedness. To be economically redundant is, paradoxically, to be subject to market forces at their most primitive. In such a context, dealing drugs makes perfect economic sense.

The spirituality of economics

In a recent survey people living in poverty were asked to describe their experience. This is what they said:

- 'powerless'
- 'isolated'
- 'degraded'
- 'angry – it's totally fixable'
- 'it's a desired condition, not an accident; it's in someone's interest that people are poor'
- 'lack of control'
- 'you're a scapegoat when there's no war or external enemy'
- 'scrutinized and judged'
- 'hopelessness and helplessness'

- 'not just about money'
- 'survival'
- 'not able to live as human beings'
- 'people take over your life (council, etc.)'
- 'in poverty, people are not needed'
- 'strain on family life'.[2]

It's noticeable that these are words about spirituality, about the effect of poverty on the human spirit.

'People don't choose to be poor or to live in poverty. In most cases it is through a series of circumstances; illness, death, unemployment or disability. So people should not feel stigmatised – yet they very often are.'[3] These words are a profound statement about value. People's sense of their own worth is today inextricably linked with the economic. We have, all of us to some degree, internalized our extrinsic market valuation.

Many of the relationships which shaped people's spirituality in the past – to land, work, community, clan or family, religion or ideology – have been subjected to a breaking process. Many of the familiar markers and signposts have disappeared or been discredited. But even when disconnected from them, the yearning for these things remains. In that loss, that void, much has been thrown on to other things to fill the gap, to restore meaning and belonging and identity; things like extremist religious or nationalist or racist ideologies, sexuality, celebrity.

Above all, the marketplace constantly entices us to find meaning, belonging and identity in the gratification of our desires through economic consumption. Whether our hungers are really satisfied in this way is debatable. Research and high levels of mental distress suggest that we are not any happier; in fact we are more anxious. What is sure is that the cost of economic growth is huge, and is unequally borne by the poorest and most vulnerable. The damage to the earth's ecology is already well known, and in the long term renders everyone deeply insecure.

So in this commodified world, I want to go back to my definition of spirituality, and apply it to our dominant economic system. I want to ask these questions:

- What is its profoundest motivation?
- What is its ultimate concern?
- What kind of choices and actions does it make and take?
- What is the nature of its relationships?

You will have your own thoughts about the answers to these questions. But I believe they are legitimate questions to ask. No longer is it possible to act as if what we do with our money has got nothing to do with our spirituality – it has everything to do with it, for where your treasure is, there will your heart be also.

In trying to understand any spirituality, it is important to look at what it believes to be its highest value. We might be of the opinion that greed, and the unbridled pursuit of profit, most characterize our economic system, but we will fail in our search for enlightenment if we do not also try to catch a glimpse of what for many is its best vision, its treasure. This I understand to be the maximization of individual *freedom*, expressed through the increased extension of *choice*. Such freedom – to own or possess, to develop and explore and utilize, to reap the rewards of one's labour and enjoy its fruits – have, it might be argued, driven the onward progress of science, technology, the arts, civic and political life, health and education, all that seems to make life worth living.

To be free, unbounded, without constraint or limitation has a huge emotional and spiritual attraction. Part of the nature of freedom is the readiness to take on board the risks that go along with it. Exploration of new territory involves the danger of getting lost, encountering unknown obstacles – the mythological cultures of the Promised Land, the Wild West, Space, the Final Frontier, recognize and accept this. Speaking at the Columbia memorial service, George W. Bush said: 'Each of these astronauts had the daring and discipline required of their calling. Each of them knew that great endeavours are insepar- able from great risk, and accepted those risks willingly in the cause of discovery.'[4] More prosaically, it is recognized in the markets, in the small print that reminds us that interest rates can go down as well as up. But in the real world of economics, the nature of freedom is also, increasingly, being perverted.

In theory, we trade the security of communal provision for individual freedom and choice. In theory, we thereby exchange the constraints placed on our actions for the risks engendered by our individual freedoms. But that trade-off is becoming less and less real. Increasingly, the risks are paid for by the same people who still suffer the constraints. Only now, not only do they not enjoy the freedom, they don't have the security either, because our free market really has got nothing to do with freedom.

At present, trading (the most reliable way to overcome poverty) is seriously distorted by such inequitable practices as the offloading of European and American surpluses on to African and South American markets, thus putting local pro- ducers out of business. Heavily subsidised western goods lower prices to such an extent that local traders simply cannot com- pete. Stringent regulations placed by western-controlled bodies like the World Trade Organization, the International Monetary Fund and the World Bank on trade and markets in developing countries, such as not allowing subsidies, are not observed by the very countries which impose them. It's a question of 'do what we say, not what we do'.

There's one area in which Britain really is a world leader – our (heavily subsidised) arms trade. Every year, half a million people across the world are killed by guns which can be bought in some places for the price of a chicken. It's estimated that there are some 100 million guns circulating in Africa alone.

The worst impact is borne by innocent civilians – children, women, the sick and elderly. Bullets claim more lives in Africa than such major killers as tuberculosis, malaria or road accidents. Firearms have transformed once stable and relatively prosperous communities into medieval fiefdoms. Vast areas of countryside are abandoned as millions flee their homes in terror; schools close, hospitals shut; ordinary life grinds to a standstill. Economic and social development has been stripped away. There are huge profits in selling guns – but the most vulnerable pay a high price.

Our government recently sold Tanzania, one of the world's poorest countries, a £28-million military radar system, though a civilian one would have cost a tenth of the price. Despite its adverse impact on sustainable development, and against massive opposition, Tony Blair gave the sale the green light.

The markets are not free. Labour is most certainly not free to move – to be an economic migrant is to be the lowest of the low, although such people are merely following the logic of the market. Only the unchecked flow of capital is free. Meanwhile, boardroom payoffs with golden pension deals to failed managers and directors go on unchecked, while the pensions of ordinary people disappear like snow off a dyke.

The areas for the exercise of our freedom are being increasingly reduced, as everything is commodified – our time, our health, our sexuality, the air that we breathe and the water that we drink, our planet itself. A freedom that is unable to take its risks upon itself is ultimately one that destroys itself. Freedom, we discover, is only meaningful within limits. A system that only recognizes extrinsic value gradually strips us of all the things that we believe have intrinsic worth.

If, as a Christian, I believe in a relationship that unconditionally values every person regardless of status, wealth, success or virtue, that conveys intrinsic worth on the worst as well as the best, with no value addition necessary, how am I to regard an economic system, and its underlying spirituality, which determines worth purely by external market forces, which relieves people who are poor, disabled, unemployed, single parents, elderly, of their intrinsic worth? We take care of what we value. Ultimately, people know whether and how they are valued by their society, and by its systems and institutions. Who do we give value to?

Speaking in South Africa, Archbishop Njongonkulu Ndungane said that:

> it is wrong and unacceptable for some people to have much, much more than they need, and others to suffer the cries of hungry children ... economics should be in the service of compassion and civilized values ... there is no intrinsic value in the accumulation of money and possessions; and these are positively harmful to humanity's spirit if they coexist with poverty.[5]

A spiritual task of inclusion

When social inclusion nowadays depends on the economic – we are what we spend, and if you can't spend, you're excluded – it is vital that people are not also excluded politically and culturally. Perhaps the starkest statements of exclusion come in the consistent experience of people living in poverty that being poor results in being regarded and treated with disrespect. Stigma, patronage, even criminalization are commonplace for people living in poverty. Along with that goes isolation. Poverty is an isolating experience wherever a person is, and being poor in a poor community doesn't necessarily guarantee solidarity.

Archbishop Ndungane again:

> Economics is linked to the kind of people a society produces. A compassionate economics produces compassionate people. A highly competitive economics produces insecure, frightened people hoarding their possessions, or aggressive people who win at the expense of other people. For those who cannot actively participate economically,

the results are poverty, crime, destruction and ultimately death.[6]

People take care of what they value. If you want to know what someone really values, look at what they take care of. And people also assess their own value and worth by the care they see being taken with and about them. 'God so loved the world', says John's Gospel, 'that he sent his only son . . .' A world where everyone matters is really about who we value, and how that shows up.

2

Sharing the blessing

The story of Jacob and his brother Esau bestrides the Hebrew scriptures like a colossus. Even today, its psychic power casts a long shadow over human history. You remember these children of Isaac and Rebecca, struggling together in the womb before they were born, Esau coming out with Jacob clutching tightly to his heel. But only one, according to the law, the elder by a breath, could inherit, and he would inherit everything. By this system, dividing property to provide equal distribution was unimaginable. It was the system by which Isaac himself had profited. His father, Abraham, had sent away all his other children so that Isaac would not be deprived of his security.

But then two things happened. First, Jacob took advantage of Esau's hunger to persuade him to trade his rights as firstborn in exchange for some food. And then, years later, Jacob, with his mother's encouragement and connivance, tricked the aged and blind Isaac into believing that he was Esau, and giving him his final dying blessing.

He [Esau] cooked some tasty food and took it to his father. . . .

'Who are you?' Isaac asked.

'Your elder son Esau,' he answered.

Isaac began to tremble and shake all over, and he asked, 'Who was it, then, who killed an animal and brought it to me? I ate it just before you came. I gave him my final blessing, and so it is his for ever.'

When Esau heard this, he cried out loudly and bitterly and said, 'Give me your blessing also, father!'

Isaac answered, 'Your brother came and deceived me. He has taken away your blessing.'

Esau said, 'This is the second time that he has cheated me. . . . He took my rights as the firstborn son and now he has taken away my blessing. Haven't you saved a blessing for me?'

Isaac answered, 'I have already made him master over you, and I have made all his relatives his slaves. I have given him corn and wine. Now there is nothing that I can do for you, my son!'

Esau continued to plead with his father, 'Have you only one blessing, father? Bless me too, father!' He began to cry.   (Genesis 27.31–38)

Now Esau hated Jacob, and planned to kill him once their father had died. So Rebecca sent Jacob away, beyond Esau's reach, for, she said, 'Why should I lose both my sons on the same day?' Esau stayed at home, let his anger cool, and to please his father, the man who could not give him his blessing, took a Hebrew wife.

Genesis 32—33 describes the meeting of Jacob and Esau after many years. Messengers had already told Jacob that Esau was coming to meet him with four hundred men, and Jacob is worried and frightened. He sends servants ahead of him with gifts, which they are to present to Esau humbly, with the words, 'These are from your servant Jacob. He sends them as a present to his master Esau.' Jacob thinks, 'I will win him over with the gifts, and when I meet him, perhaps he will forgive me' (Genesis 32.20).

And so Jacob goes out with all his family to meet Esau. We read:

Jacob went ahead of them and bowed down to the ground seven times as he approached his brother. But Esau ran to meet him, threw his arms around him and kissed him. They were both crying. . . .

[Esau asks Jacob about the gifts.] Jacob answered, 'It was to gain your favour.'

But Esau said: 'I have enough, my brother; keep what you have.'

Jacob replied: 'No, please, if I have gained your favour, accept my gift. To see your face is for me like seeing the face of God, now that you have been so friendly to me.'

(Genesis 33.3–4, 8–10)

Our scriptures, our faith, our Lord, all teach us that blessing is first and foremost communal blessing, a birthright for all of abundance, of enough when what is provided is shared. In the story of Jacob and Esau, we are presented with blessing misappropriated and abused, taken from being a communal inheritance to be a prize in a game for winners and losers; the prize being the right to function in the image of the god of monopoly who alone held all power in his hands. And when blessing is reduced to being a prize in a game, it becomes extremely difficult for those who wish to claim their share of the inheritance to do so outside the rules of the game. In their different ways, Isaac, Rebecca and Jacob were all limited in their response to this palpable injustice, this departure from right relationship.

According to the rules of the game, not only could Isaac not give an additional blessing to Esau, he was required to condemn him for being a loser, and then he was obliged to curse the loser. In this game, you are not debarred for cheating – cheating becomes a tactic for winning. There is no way to restore justice to the one wronged. And in order to live with oneself, it then becomes necessary to find a way of making the loser to blame for losing. The loser must deserve to lose. Otherwise we must question the game itself – and who wants to do that when you're the winner?

And Rebecca? Well, in this game, she wasn't even allowed to be a participant on her own behalf. She could only exercise power through her son. Throwing all her frustrated ingenuity in on Jacob's side, they won. But the cost of victory for Rebecca was that she betrayed her elder son, endured twenty years of separation from the younger one, and died unattended by him, on whom she had bet all of herself. He was away playing the next round. In the patriarchal game, her choice lay between being a loser or a collaborator.

And what about the winner? Twenty years on, he is inhibited, guilt-ridden, ever more cautious, anxious and fearful of Esau, always planning and plotting, the consequences, one feels, of stealing a birthright. And when they meet, it is Esau, the one who has been cheated out of his inheritance, who is generous-hearted and forgiving, spontaneous in expressing his feelings and faithful to his human needs. Where Isaac had felt himself bound by the rules of the game, Esau believed otherwise. By ignoring its rules and acting according to more open and merciful values, he, of all of them, was able to transcend the game.

The word 'transcend' literally means 'to climb above or beyond', and transcendence is usually associated with that which is exalted, out of reach. But perhaps in order to transcend the monopoly game, we have to go in the other direction, and come right down to earth, as Esau did. He transcended the limitations of the game by remaining absolutely rooted, engaged in the daily concerns of his land and family, by refusing to accept the split between a high and holy god who was powerless to extend blessing, and the wronged and dispossessed who sought it. Esau continued to act in solidarity with the God who intends life abundant for everyone. He disregarded that god far away from people. That god in the sky has been held up ever since as a threat to people who refuse to accept their allotted role as losers in the monopoly game.

George MacLeod, reflecting on the god in the sky, said that the question that the wise men and shepherds, the seekers after truth and the followers of stars are asking us now is: how far above the things of earth is Christ at God's right hand? And he quotes Studdert Kennedy in reply:

> As far as meaning is from speech,
>   As beauty from a rose,
> As far as music is from sound,
>   As poetry from prose, . . .
>
> As far as love from friendship is,
>   As reason is from Truth,
> As far as laughter is from joy,
>   And early years from youth,
> As far as love from shining eyes,
>   As passion from a kiss,
> So far is God from God's green earth,
>   So far that world from this.[1]

It is, he said, an incarnate word that must be spoken.

In the tortured familial relationships of this great story, we can see the tortured familial relationships of our time, our communities, our world; here is the human family. It is a timely reminder that, whatever our present-day obsessions with what the Bible may or may not say about various sexualities, its core concerns in human relationships remain those between parents and children and between siblings. And it is for me a most profound meditation on our present economic world order, and the game of winners and losers it represents.

I don't think it's overly fanciful to see parallels between Jacob, the ostensible winner, and the rich of the world, in which we must include Britain. The verdict is still out on the ability of the Make Poverty History campaign to effect significant and long-lasting change. But there is no doubt of its unparalleled success in mobilizing millions of people across the world to become more aware, to lobby, to take action for such change. Above all, it has, I think, marked a shift in the post-war consensus in rich countries, from one which sees the problem as the failure, fecklessness and general lack of 'being like us' of poorer countries, to which the solution is a mixture of punishment, patronage and charity, to one in which the problem is as much our exploitation, inequitable trade relations and racism, to which the solution is justice and sustainability.

But, as with Jacob, it's all much harder when it's close to home. Africa is so far away, the poverty so stark, the inequities so glaring that the moral case for change is obvious to any thinking person with a conscience. The solutions too are more removed, at least in theory; debt cancellation, fairer trade rules and property rights, better aid – their impact on us is mediated through many levels. But poverty at home is a different matter. Britain is one of the richest countries in the world. We do not suffer resource shortages or the impoverishing effects of war or civil conflict, and only rarely do we suffer a natural disaster. We have a stable democracy and the dominant economic system is weighted in our favour. There is no reason for anyone in this country to be poor. We do not have a problem of poverty; we have a problem of distribution. In many countries, we could say that poverty causes inequality. In Britain, inequality causes poverty. This is not Dives and Lazarus, this is Jacob and Esau.

So what was it that moved Jacob, the liar and cheat, to change?

For the sake of Rachel, the woman he loved, Jacob worked without pay for seven years, was cheated by Rachel's father Laban into marrying his other daughter Leah, then worked another seven years for Rachel, and, the Bible says, 'the time seemed like only a few days to him, because he loved her'. Perhaps in experiencing what it was like to be on the receiving end of injustice, Jacob looked at his own behaviour in a different light, and saw that the theological fault line didn't just run through other people. *People are motivated to change and act when we can make a connection between our own experience and that of others.*

Jacob's love for his family is the best part of him; for their sakes he endured much. His concern for them, based on a realistic expectation of what he might expect from Esau, led him to seek to make restitution and restore right relations with Esau. Jesus said, 'If a house is divided against itself, that house will not be able to stand' (Mark 3.25). If the members of a household are at odds with one another, if they fear and suspect each other, if their relations are not equitable, then the life of the household is tense, guarded and full of anxiety. The overall well-being of any society ultimately depends on the well-being of its most vulnerable members. *People are motivated to change and act when we see it is in the best interests of those we love.*

The story of Jacob, complex and detailed and occasionally very funny as it is as everyone engages in trickery, subterfuge and politicking, is nevertheless the story of people locked into a system that seems to offer no alternatives to bad behaviour. It is a vivid illustration of original sin, the fact that we are all born into complicity with structural injustice. Jacob did not choose the injustice he was born into, and was not responsible for it; but he *was* responsible for his continuing complicity with it. It was only at the point where he chose to refuse further collusion, and sought a different basis for his relations with Esau that he acted freely as someone taking responsibility for his actions. When Jacob went out to meet Esau, he knew he could not undo the original theft. But he was not paralysed by what he could not do. He did what he could, not what he couldn't. It is important to have our complicity in the structures of injustice by which we profit made explicit. But it is not enough. Our complicity is so immense, we are so tangled up in its web, that we can end up completely disempowered. We need to know that every act of resistance to complicity, however small, makes a difference, cuts a strand in the tangle, creates alternatives, and also strengthens our capacity to act freely. *People are motivated to change and act when we believe even small changes, small actions, can make a difference.*

Jacob took a big risk in going to meet Esau. But in the years since they had met, perhaps his perception of what it meant to share a birthright had altered. My dictionary gives three meanings for the word 'share'. First, 'to distribute or apportion', with its strong suggestion of power, of who has the right to determine who shall get a share, and of what size. In my dictionary, this meaning is illustrated by the phrase, 'to share out food and clothing to the poor'. This is the Isaac understanding. The second meaning for 'sharing' is 'the dividing or cutting off part of what one has, and giving it to another or others'. It is to give away some, and to have less oneself. It is a diminishment. This is the Rebecca understanding.

The third, and last, meaning my dictionary gives is 'to enjoy in common with others, to participate'. This is the Esau understanding. The first two meanings focus on the thing being shared, the third on the people it is being shared with. Between these two lines in a dictionary lies all the difference in the world.

Perhaps Jacob changed when sharing started to become more about the possibility of communal joys than about control or diminution. We ourselves have less experience than in the past of having to rely on others, of having a pleasure enhanced by sharing it, of seeing ourselves as an interdependent part of others, and all our politics and economics are exacerbating this trend. Such is the competitive nature of the market now that it becomes ever harder to engage in a demanding common task in which co-operation is both a necessity and a joy. Skills, knowledge and information are increasingly commodities to be competitively traded and jealously guarded. Because we have lost confidence in our capacity to make and sustain relationships, it is easier not to risk the attempt – and there are many substitutes now available to protect us, to ensure that we need have less and less connection with the people who suffer on the sharp end of our inequalities, and who are consistently demonized and discriminated against. Rediscovering the communal joys is one of the gifts of community, for here, where we take the risk of breaking open our isolation and self-justification, of going forward to meet Esau, we discover not condemnation and rejection, but generosity, acceptance and a new relationship. *People are motivated to change and act when we believe that justice is both served by and results in communal joys.*

The night before he goes to meet Esau, Jacob, quite alone and still on his endless, human quest for blessing, wrestles till daybreak with one who comes to him. He receives his blessing, but limps away wounded. And in this adversary, perhaps that part of the self we all struggle with in the tension between acting freely and justly and our own limitations and self-interest, Jacob sees the face of God.

And you remember that Jacob came bearing gifts for Esau, seeking to win back his favour and his own safe passage. But Esau did not need the kind of gifts Jacob offered. We always risk offering inappropriate and ultimately self-seeking gifts, and we cannot conduct our economic affairs as if they were spiritual exercises, offering patronage, charity or advanced spiritual awareness in return for misappropriated blessing. Jacob discovered that in Esau also he saw the face of God. *People are motivated to change and act when we can see the face of God in our deepest struggles and in those we have wronged.*

Our resistance to complicity, our refusal to play by the rules of the game of winners and losers, has to be embodied in our priorities and programmes, in our work and in our lives, as it was in Jesus. We are seeking to restore a birthright misappropriated, to share more equitably an original blessing. That is not to say we have to refuse the blessing. But we live in the tension of affirming the blessing while refusing the privatization which diminishes it. That personal and political tension can only be embraced where we are. And at the end of his long life, Isaac was buried by both of his sons together.

3

Bambalela: Never give up

In summer 2006 I was in South Africa, visiting a church in the township of Guguletu outside Cape Town with which the Iona Community has a partnership. Above the door of the sanctuary, so that people see it as they leave worship, are the words, 'Never give up'. And the congregation have a song, '*Bambalela*: never give up', which is regularly sung there in worship.

They need to sing it a lot, because this is a church with a huge mission and a huge heart, facing huge challenges. In a population of 300,000 in Guguletu around 30 per cent are infected with HIV. In the desperate poverty in which so many black South Africans live, treatment and good nutrition are often not available. There are many orphans and vulnerable children. In the midst of poverty, unemployment and illness, the people in Guguletu are living every day on the threshold between life and death.

But these are not people who give up easily, and in J. L. Zwane Presbyterian Church, they live hopefully. Every day, hundreds receive a cooked meal, others receive monthly food parcels. There are numerous support and counselling groups for people living with HIV, and for their families and children, and a team of home-carers. Others receive palliative care through a day hospice.

An after-school study programme is attended each day by 130 children, where they have a chance to have a meal, do homework, and receive additional study support, essential for children living in overcrowded homes with no electricity.

The centre has trained over three thousand people as HIV/AIDS educators. It runs a clinic in an informal settlement. It's involved in a rural outreach programme in the Eastern Cape, where a bakery, chicken farming, gardening, pig farming, forestry and an HIV/AIDS awareness programme have been established.

It has a sports development programme for under-13s, helping them to develop positive life skills. It started Siyaya, a performing group which does HIV/AIDS education through music and reaches hundreds in Guguletu each week.

During worship each Sunday a person who is HIV-positive shares their story. (Can you imagine that happening week by week in your local congregation?) Yet to mention some of the many activities associated with this prophetic ministry is not really to describe what goes on there day by day. It is the work of the gospel, mediated through women and men who have been touched by the Spirit, and who, wounded and weary themselves, humbly companion the wounded and weary. Almost every person who works there is a volunteer.

You would think that this kind of ministry would find universal affirmation and encouragement. Is it not putting the gospel into practice? I thought so. But, in fact, the church has attracted controversy and even disapproval for its work, because it welcomes everyone affected by HIV/AIDS. The minister of the church explained it this way:

It is about people meeting people, listening to what they are going through and attempting to figure out where God is in all this. We have to try to walk with them. As a congregation we consciously decided to invite, embrace, include and engage people living with and affected by HIV/AIDS.[1]

Like this man, who said, 'I think I've at least six things going against me these days. I'm poor; I'm unemployed; I'm

HIV-positive; I've had my legs amputated; I'm black and I'm gay.'[2]

He found a welcome at the J. L. Zwane church, but one woman in a different church was not so fortunate:

> I used to attend the local church but I don't any more. The pastor there believes that you can't be a Christian and have HIV. Two of my friends from the church used to keep telling me not to take any medicines, just to trust in Jesus to heal me. I couldn't accept that. I want to have Jesus and keep taking medicines. So I don't go to church any more, but I pray every morning for my family, for my son, for the doctors and everyone living with HIV/AIDS.[3]

Within South Africa, and beyond, there is still a huge stigma attached to being HIV-positive. Many pastors in the churches continue to regard HIV/AIDS, which is so much linked to poverty and marginalization, as a fierce judgement from God on human sin and they reject people who are HIV-positive, an understanding which has caused endless suffering to thousands.

Well, we are in no position to stand in judgement on these churches; how many of our churches offer a real, dignified, *unconditional* welcome to people who are poor, unemployed, HIV-positive, disabled, black, gay, a welcome that is not shot through with judgement, the belief that 'we know what's best for them'? When I was in Guguletu, a student from one of America's most famous theological seminaries, working in an affluent white Cape Town church, came to visit for a day. At the end of the day, having seen all that was being done, he said to one of the volunteers, 'This is all very well, but you are not preaching the gospel here. You are not telling the people about Jesus.'

I cannot tell you how angry and sad this comment made me. Aside altogether from the extreme western arrogance of spending a few hours somewhere and presuming you know enough about it to pass judgement, it made me wonder deeply about the kind of Christianity he believed in.

A time for repentance

A few years ago, I visited a place called Elmina as part of a large international Christian pilgrimage. Elmina Castle is one of the slave fortresses on the coast of Ghana in West Africa, built by the Portuguese, then held by the Dutch and the British in turn, which held those who had been abducted and captured into slavery, as they suffered in dungeons waiting for slave ships that would take them to unknown lands and destinies. Over four brutal centuries, 15 million African slaves were transported to the Americas, and millions more were captured and died. On this trade in humans as commodities, wealth in Europe was built. Through their labour, sweat, suffering, intelligence and creativity, the wealth of the Americas was developed.

At the Elmina Castle, the European merchants, soldiers, and Governor lived on the upper level, while the slaves were held in captivity one level below. We entered a room used as a church, with words from Psalm 132 on a sign still hanging above the door ('For the Lord has chosen Zion . . .'). And we imagined Christians worshipping their God while directly below them, right under their feet, those being sold into slavery suffered in chains. This awful travesty was a very ecumenical one, played out in turn by Catholic Christians, Reformed Christians and Anglican Christians.

In angry bewilderment we thought, 'How could their faith be so divided from life? How could their faith be so blind?'

Some of us who were there were descendants of those who were enslaved – African Americans from North America, from the Caribbean, from South America. Others of us were descended from those slave-traders and slave-owners, if not directly, then as citizens of countries which were hugely complicit in it. We shared responses of tears, silence, anger and lamentation.

When I returned home from Ghana, I read about the involvement of Scots in the slave trade, and discovered that in the eighteenth century, one-third of the land of Jamaica was owned by Scots, and run as sugar plantations worked by African slaves.

Christians have always declared God's sovereignty over all life and all the earth. So how could these forebears in faith deny so blatantly in their actions what they proclaimed so loudly in their words? How could they look at Jesus and see the dungeons of Elmina? Or, how could they look at Jesus and see apartheid? Or, perhaps, how can they look at Jesus and see five hundred dead children in Lebanon?

It has always been easy for Christians to overlook Jesus when it suits their interests, helped by some very bad theology, and the ability to be deeply, and sometimes quite peculiarly, selective in biblical interpretation. Apartheid, for example, drew theological justification for its abhorrent practices from a few obscure verses in the Hebrew Bible, while seemingly oblivious to everything that Jesus said, taught and lived. And hand in hand with the tendency to render Jesus invisible has been the capacity also to make invisible, or disposable, or less than fully human, those whose existence offended, or threatened vested interests.

Slavery was promoted and practised by good upstanding Christians who argued that black Africans did not have a soul, were less human than white Europeans, and therefore could be treated inhumanly. Indeed, many argued that it was their destiny and duty to bear the white man's burden and rule over people of colour. This is not a belief that has disappeared. I heard it said in South Africa by white people for whom apartheid lives on in their divided minds: 'They don't place the same value on human life as we do.' This came from the people who shot down five hundred children in Soweto. I hear it said about Muslims.

The year 2007 marked the bicentenary of the abolition of the British slave trade, and there were many books, television programmes and articles about this long and bitterly contested campaign. Both Bristol and Liverpool, cities deeply involved in the Atlantic slave trade, had major events taking place, and a new museum was dedicated to the history of slavery in Liverpool. It is important that the commemorations help us to reflect not just on the achievements of the abolitionists, heroic and persistent though they undoubtedly were, but on centuries of complicity in slavery by Britain, on the still unaccounted-for profits that accrued to this country from it, and the huge cost that others paid for our prosperity. Otherwise the commemorations run the risk of being the self-justifications of a society which is guilty but without repentance and restitution.

And we who are Christians might spend some time thinking about all the times Christians got it catastrophically, shamefully wrong – about slavery, apartheid, colonialism, about the murder of thousands of women as witches. Wrong about Galileo, about leprosy, about HIV/AIDS, about the status of women. I don't forget that:

> If we had to wait for the churches to promote tertiary education for women, the Married Woman's Property Act, the franchise, entry to the professions, equal pay for equal work, the Sex Discrimination Act, and many other measures vital to women's health and wellbeing, we should still be waiting. Indeed, the churches frequently opposed such reforms.[4]

The Bible is full of stories of violence against women: they are commonplace, of women gang-raped, subjected to incest, mutilated, silenced, trafficked, enslaved, murdered. And yet . . . the most frightening thing about these stories is not the fate of the women, terrible though that was. It is that no one in the stories as they are told cares about the women; their suffering is not regarded with compassion or regret. There is no loyalty or tenderness towards them, no care for them. They do not matter.

The only offence considered is that given to the honour of the men to whom they were attached.

It has taken the Christian church nigh on two thousand years to notice that no one cared about these women. This is our holy book, but we have read it with blinkers. We have read it as if Jesus never lived. We have read it, women too, through the eyes of men, and it has materially affected the ways that women have been treated for centuries.

This disordered relationship with scripture shows up all over the place. I couldn't count the number of people who have spoken to me, weeping in fear and confusion because they have been threatened into a literalist understanding of the Bible which is profoundly selective, and which goes against every stirring of conscience and every instinct of humanity and all that they encounter in Jesus. They have experienced scripture as a manifesto to wave, or even a weapon to be used to hurt and maim and exclude. The failure to read the scriptures with discernment, recognizing what is historical, what poetic, what devotional and what contextual, what is life-giving and what is simply toxic, has done untold damage to millions, and, not least, to the Bible itself. Instead of being the book of life, it has become to millions the book of death, dripping with blood.

The myth of redemptive violence

You might think that, having got so much wrong so very badly, a bit of humility and restraint might not be out of place, a willingness to hear the plea . . . 'consider it possible that you may be mistaken'. But no, manifest destiny must be fulfilled. The white man's burden must be shouldered once again. We must polish up the myth of redemptive violence.

I admire the resilience and courage of Londoners after the July 7 bombings in 2005. It's entirely right that it should have been recognized and applauded. But the city of Baghdad has experienced the equivalent of the London bombings almost every day since then! Their resilience and courage have won no awards or honours or tabloid articles. Why should that be? Is it because we truly believe that the horrors they endure are for their own good?

The myth of redemptive violence, the notion that hurting and killing people is good for them, has exerted, and continues to exert, huge power. This myth authorizes the beating of children, often by religious people, 'for their own good', the subordination of women, because they are 'weaker', the oppression of whole peoples because they are 'inferior' or 'uncivilized', occupation, imperialism, colonialism and neocolonialism. It is the authorization for British and US policy in Iraq. Just as much as Islamic terror, it depends on the myth of religiously sanctioned redemptive violence.

This myth saves people from having to engage with the central humanitarian value that people are not expendable as a means to an end, and leaves fundamental abuses of power unchallenged. That is why it is necessary. It raises violence to the status of a virtue. It justifies hateful and unjust means. It instrumentalizes young people as weapons. It serves the killers, not the killed. It is particularly useful when other interests are at stake as well – markets, resource flows, arms sales, political campaigns at home.

The myth of redemptive violence relies on being able to blur the distinction between a just cause and a just war. It matters to countries going to war that it be seen to be a moral war, a just war; otherwise, what authority is there for it and in what way are we different from and superior to those we fight? But the classical theory of the just war underlines much of the ambiguity about that distinction. The conditions justifying a war have been established as follows: the war must be defensive and a response to unjust aggression; all other methods of resolving the conflict must have been exhausted; there must be a realistic chance of success to justify all the wartime sacrifices; there must be some proportion between the moral and physical costs of the hostilities and the peace and better social order sought afterwards; only military targets, not unarmed civilians, can be the targets of military strikes; force may never be used as a means in itself or to brutalize the social order and the military personnel. I do not think it now possible for modern warfare to meet these conditions. It certainly didn't in Iraq or Lebanon.

We are in mortal danger of repeating the same sin of those slave-traders whose blindness we decry. For the world is still divided between those who worship in comfortable contentment and those enslaved by the world's economic injustice, ideological violence and ecological destruction, who still suffer and die. The world is still under the shadow of an oppressive empire, the gathered power of pervasive economic and political forces across the globe that reinforce the division between rich and poor. Millions of people, including Christians, live daily in the midst of these realities. Meanwhile, millions of others in our Christian congregations live lives as inattentive to this suffering as those who worshipped God in the room above slave dungeons.

This goes to the heart of our confession of faith. How can we say that we believe that Jesus Christ is the Lord of life, and not stand against all that denies the promise of fullness of life to the world? Or is our faith one of Christianity for dead people? Is it a matter of adhering to a series of rules and propositions, an insurance policy for the hereafter? Is it about embracing a feel-good, lifestyle spirituality that allows us to live accommodated to our death-dealing world order, which lets us sing hymns in our upstairs chapel in the fortress deaf to the cries from the slave dungeons below? Do we think the gospel call to mission is answered by signing people up to the Jesus club while leaving the door of the dungeons firmly locked, by telling them that what's really important is what happens to them once they're dead? Well, it certainly lets us off the hook of any kind of responsibility for their *lives*! This is Christianity for dead people! And it's why the Christian Aid slogan is so important, so challenging and so truthful to the gospel – 'We believe in life before death.'

Or is it perhaps that we are the enslaved ones as the divisions in the world between rich and poor, powerful and powerless, grow sharper, are characterized by increasing violence and insecurity and seek to isolate us from one another? Perhaps that's why it's easier to turn away from confronting all of that to bread and circuses, to chemically induced oblivion and reality TV shows, or, for some religious people, to the huge threat to human society apparently posed by gay people.

Doing things differently

But is it not the case that the spirit of Jesus requires and invites us to belong more deeply to one another, to challenge and overcome those divisions through that spirit? Is this not what the call to conversion, to transformation of life is all about?

We are all born into complicity, part of an oppressive, dehumanizing world order into which we have been born, and for which we did not give our permission. This is original sin, our separation from one another and from God. But by the grace and generosity of God, we are forgiven and set free to be responsible; responsible for the complicity we *do* have a choice about. We can say, 'This is the way things are – but I beg to differ.' Jesus invited his followers to do things differently.

Of course that's very hard, because it's not our default position, and it's always a minority position. But it's no harder than it was for the few people who started the campaign for an end to slavery, who were also up against powerful vested interest and the love of money. Or for the Glasgow Presbytery of the Church of Scotland, who, in 1792, in a city whose whole prosperity was built on slavery, voted for the abolition of the slave trade. It's not as hard as it is for the people in Guguletu. There are ways for every one of us, even small ways, to be dissenters. We can make a noise, and refuse to say prayers while beneath

35

us people rot in dungeons – and we can tell our political and church leaders so.

When the women went to the grave of the crucified Jesus and could not find his body, the angels said to the women, 'Why do you look for the living among the dead? He is not here. He is alive.' It is a paradox of the good news that fullness of life is found in embracing those very realities that we fear most, in confronting our fears, in dying and rising into the glorious freedom of the children of God. But that freedom, and the joy and hope it brings, are not to be found in intellectual assent or theorizing, or in better techniques for prayer. They are found in engagement, in the midst of people, in the midst of all the hurt and shame and vulnerability we share with all human beings everywhere.

One South African living with HIV said this:

> We cannot escape our grief or the losses we have experi-
> enced. But we can act to minimise this suffering, to pre-
> vent further deaths, to open our hearts and hold in them
> those who, now, are afflicted with illness and its isolation.
> We cannot allow our bereavement to inflict a further loss
> upon us: the loss of our own full humanity, our capacity
> to feel and respond and support. We must incorporate
> our grief into our everyday living, by turning it into an
> energy for living, by exerting ourselves as never before.
> AIDS beckons us to the fullness and power of our own
> humanity. It is not an invitation that we should avoid or
> refuse.[5]

And here is Spiwo Xapile, the minister of the J. L. Zwane church where they have accepted that invitation:

> There are many things to celebrate here in Guguletu.
> There is LIFE here. There is talent here. Sometimes that
> life and talent lie dormant. There is a temptation to con-
> centrate on death and dying. But we also need to help

people to embrace life in its fullness. There is not only life in Guguletu, there is also a lot of love and respect in this community. I tell people here how wonderful and good they are and that affirms them to move forward. There is enough judgement around, not just in the churches![6]

I wanted to send this prayer, written in Xhosa by a member of one of the HIV/AIDS support groups, to the American theology student who visited Guguletu. I hoped it would help him to understand. I invite you to listen to Noma-lady's words, and to walk with her and many others as a sister or brother. We belong together.

God is love to me, and God is amazing even though I am not strong physically in terms of my health. Even though things are difficult I continue to go down on my knees and pray, and from time to time I see God responding to my prayer. I don't know how I could praise God's name in a way that is befitting God's greatness. I do not have the instruments appropriate enough to make the music that would truly express how I feel about God. There are times when I have sleepless nights and watch TV till morning, but I always feel comfort when I go on my knees and pray. I am sometimes up at 3 a.m. trying to sleep on that side or the other. There are times when the pain is so heavy: my hand with cramps; my fingers twisting. Had I not been connected with God I would be accusing people of causing this pain, but earlier in my life I chose a close relationship with God, though I am poor. God is with me in the morning when I wake up: God is around during sleep, and is with me as I try to walk around. I just cry knowing that God has heard my prayer. I live with great hope. Amen.[7]

Bambalela – never give up!

4

Living with difference

A few years ago, I visited Bosnia with a group of British Christians and Muslims. One of the most interesting aspects of the visit for me was discovering an indigenous, white community that had been Muslim for centuries. They were not migrants or refugees, they were as European as I was, and they shared the same concerns, aspirations and values. It was an important lesson; I realized how many of the assumptions I make about Islam had been shaped by my experience of the Scottish Muslim community, which mostly originated in Pakistan, and how many of them were primarily cultural rather than religious. It also gave me a renewed sense of the rich diversity of Europe, and how little we appreciate it. Though we go to considerable lengths now to protect bio-diversity, we are not so good at engaging with cultural diversity, and European history is somewhat compromised in this regard.

In every country in the world one of the major challenges of the twenty-first century is 'How shall we live with difference?' We must find ways to live together in peace, though we are different, because there are no good alternatives. We have seen the way of separation and division: in Northern Ireland, behind the ironically titled 'peace lines'; in the Balkans; in apartheid South Africa; in Israel and the Occupied Palestinian Territories. This is not a good alternative. We have seen the way of ethnic cleansing, of warfare, of genocide. This is an even worse alternative, a many-headed hydra that breeds more death.

We are people of faith, and our vision is of better alternatives. How shall we live, not fearfully but with the glorious freedom of the children of God? Where are our resources for resistance and persistence in our faith? I want to reflect on three stories of biblical women who took on responsibility for shaping alternatives.

Stories of exile and return

Beside the streams of Babylon, we sat ourselves and
  wept,
Remembering the land we loved, and all the hope it
  kept.[1]

The experience of exile is part of the Scottish collective memory. When God-fearing Highland Scots were cleared from their homes and livelihoods in the nineteenth century by landlords who saw more profit in sheep and sporting estates than in a subsistence peasant economy, tens of thousands of them took ship for North America. They were sometimes hastened on their way by collusive clergy, who told them that their suffering was God's punishment for their sinful ways. Not for the first time, the interests of God and the interests of Mammon were conveniently conflated. In the process, families were separated, usually for ever, traditional ways of life were destroyed and the web of life was torn.

These economic migrants made lengthy, dangerous and squalid journeys to find a new and better life for themselves and their families. Our attitude to those who went this way, not only from Scotland but from England, Wales and Ireland also, is interesting. We think of them as brave, resourceful, heroic even. We are compassionate towards the plight that led them to leave – the famines, clearances, poverty and destitution – and we sing about the pain of leaving loved ones, and about the hardships they endured in the new world. And when their descendants return to the old country to visit, we rightly welcome them with open arms and praise their achievements and their prosperity; the towns and cities they founded, the businesses they built up, the churches they planted as they took their faith with them. We believe that they had no alternative but to go, and we are proud of what they did.

Our great-great-grandparents sang the same psalms of exile and return as the people of Israel, as refugees, exiles and forced migrants have done in many times and places. In this poetry we can hear the lament and the longing for a beloved land; but also the rage of powerlessness against the oppressors, as a reading of Psalm 137 vividly demonstrates.

In another biblical narrative of exile and return, Ruth is a foreigner in Israel, a lone woman. Her economic situation is precarious in the extreme; seeking to provide for herself and her mother-in-law, an Israelite whose life and faith Ruth has identified with, and whom she has served unstintingly, Ruth goes to gather leftover corn from harvested fields. Here, Ruth is at her most vulnerable. Being the people of God obviously does not inhibit the Israelite men from feeling at liberty to molest a woman alone! Naomi suggests that sleeping with Boaz, her wealthy male relative, is for Ruth's own good. 'This will bring you security'; Naomi sends Ruth to Boaz's bed to trade with her only possession, her own body, knowing that if there is any security to come from it, she, Naomi, will also take a share in it. And if it all goes wrong . . . well, Naomi is spared those consequences; after all, Ruth is a Moabite!

The book of Ruth is often described as a gentle and peaceful one, preceded as it is by the extreme gender violence of the book of Judges. But it isn't really. Its apparently good ending not only masks the question of what happened to all the other foreign women who did not find a Boaz, but it can also lead us to overlook what happens to people who are powerless in the face of intransigent social systems.

This was a period in post-exilic Israelite history of vicious legislation against inter-ethnic marriage, of Gentile women and their children summarily divorced and abandoned. Furthermore, Moabite women in particular are stigmatized as sexually promiscuous and idolatrous. And yet this Moabite is in every respect faithful, loving and loyal.

Ruth is exposed, the alien who must prove herself to find even a modicum of acceptance. Above all, Ruth is the supplicant. She must humble herself, throw herself on another's mercy and ask for help. The need to be a supplicant has not, of course, disappeared. It is a reality that characterizes significant aspects of international relations, especially economic relations; it is the experience of asylum-seekers and refugees; it is still the experience of millions of women across the world, and it seeps into the experience of those whose difference or minority status make it almost unavoidable. It is the experience today of many poor countries.

To be a supplicant is something that contemporary western culture finds intolerable; especially (though not solely) for men. To receive without being able to give in return we find demeaning. Yet even in our culture of power and autonomy, the experience of being a supplicant touches us too; when ageing or illness forces us to relinquish our powers; when unemployment or family crisis or personal injury removes them, or simply when we find ourselves in situations completely beyond our control. Perhaps one of the reasons we are so fearful, almost pathologically so, we who are the powerful of Europe, is that minorities, because they have no automatic belonging, must supplicate again and again, confront us with what we most fear – our own vulnerability, our own lack, our own most deep-seated failure. Far easier to anathematize them, project our fears, distance ourselves. They are the part of ourselves that we cannot bear to confront. And yet they are a part that we need in order to be wholly human.

Peter Cruchley-Jones writes:

At the end of the story, Ruth's voice is silenced. We do not hear her voice or even her name spoken. The wedding between Ruth and Boaz hints at a new covenant that has room for both Judah and Moab . . . But perhaps the absence of Ruth in the text is actually recognising the way our prejudice almost automatically reconfigures itself. Ruth really is now part of Israel, so potentially she can become invisible, and attitudes to Moab, to foreigners can remain unchecked now that she is an honorary Jew? Or is this the test the story finally sets the reader, the task to take away?[2]

Concern about minorities has been focused recently by the increased number of economic migrants, like Ruth, into Europe. I am a European. I have a European passport. My belonging is unquestioned, rooted in my colour, my nationality, my language and accent, my religion, and the fact that in all these things, I am part of a majority. I do not have to prove that I belong.

This unquestioned belonging is something that many people in Europe are unable to take for granted, even if they were born here. If they are not white, they will frequently be assumed to be foreigners, asylum-seekers or refugees, and because of their permanent visibility assumed to be present in much greater numbers than they actually are. They may speak excellent English or French or German but if their accent is not recognizably 'European', their belonging will not be unquestioned. If they are Muslim, their belonging may be particularly questioned, sometimes in threatening and hostile fashion, and may make them guilty by association. My belonging, as a Christian, on the other hand, has never been questioned as a result of the violence perpetrated by Christians in Northern Ireland, or by Christian-originated violence in Bosnia, Iraq or anywhere else in the world.

To be part of a minority, especially a visibly or audibly different one, is always to have to prove one's belonging and have no signs of proof that are ever enough. Previous generations of immigrants to Europe, attempting to belong, to assimilate like Ruth, were met by a queasy mixture of racism and exploitation of their labour. Their second- and third-generation children, perhaps more confident, or more cynical, have challenged us on our professions of democracy and individual freedoms, and asserted an identity of difference. In this, they are doing what emigrating Europeans have always done, whether that be in the mission and church-planting in Africa and South America which accompanied colonialism, or in expatriate enclaves, or in supplanting indigenous cultures altogether to become the unquestioned majority; they have carried their language, culture, religion, politics and economics, and, let us not forget, in some of these places, their military capacity with them, to create places where they could feel at home, where they could belong without always having to prove it.

How curious, then, that our attitudes to immigrants into Europe should be so different. Misunderstanding, racism, relentless hostility are daily experiences, and when the many who are Christian attend churches here, they do not always receive the welcome that our faith demands of us. The irony is that we need them as much as they need us – Scotland, for instance, has a declining, ageing population. We need the youthful energy, new ideas and skills that immigrants bring. The image of the rich countries of the world, securing their own interests and then pulling the drawbridge up behind them, of Fortress Europe, is not a very good advert for the much lauded benefits of democracy, freedom and free trade! But this is how much of the world understands Christianity.

Some years ago, the BBC screened a play about refugees coming to Europe. The last scene is vividly etched on my memory. It was of a pristine southern European beach. Up the beach were crawling dozens of ragged, exhausted figures, mostly black. On a terrace above the beach, elegantly dressed white people drank cocktails and chatted, turning away in horror from the emaciated bodies below them. The impact of the scene was powerful and unforgettable. At the time, I took it as a metaphor; today, of course, we know that this is the way many of the dispossessed arrive in Europe.

From our viewpoint on the terrace looking down at the beach (and many *are* looking, not just turning their backs) perhaps we need to think more about what it really means for us to welcome people and include them as full participants in our communities and our churches.

A woman of integrity

This challenge also faced Jesus in the second of our stories. In Matthew 15, Jesus encounters a Canaanite woman. Here is another supplicant, another outsider. But this is not a daughter acting on behalf of her mother, but a mother in despair for her daughter, seeking Jesus' intervention for the sick body and spirit of her child. We are most vulnerable through the children we love, and perhaps we supplicate most deeply on their behalf.

The story is one of only two in the Gospel in which healing is offered to a Gentile, and at a distance. This Canaanite woman, one of the indigenous and dispossessed people of Israel, is also alone, without a male to give her a name or protection. She seeks Jesus out, addresses him in the most respectful terms, and supplicates him to have mercy on her suffering child. At first Jesus ignores her, and then his disciples ask him to send this noisy woman away. But she, like other women in the Gospels, is persistent, and her need is great. She enters into dialogue with him, does not dissent from his description of her people as 'dogs', but rather redirects it and appeals to him once again as Lord. She asserts her claim and demonstrates her faith not by protesting the disdainful reference to her ethnic group, but by arguing that both Gentiles and Jews are under the same authority. Still respectful, she turns his metaphor on its head, with an astute and daring response.

44

Jesus has already demonstrated that religious custom, such as Sabbath observance, should not stand in the way of responding to human need. Now, challenged to see that social conventions should not do so either, his integrity requires him to recognize the extent of the woman's faith and to re-examine his own mission. He salutes the woman's faith, and answers her entreaty. It is from this point onwards that Jesus understands that he has been sent, not only to the people of Israel, but also to the Gentiles. The new relationship will henceforth include them.

Once again, the courage, faith and resourcefulness of a woman who takes risks and makes herself vulnerable change the shape of God's mission. We never know the woman's name, only that she was a Canaanite, that she was alone, and that she loved her daughter.

In this story, there is a crucial question of integrity. Integrity is the wholeness of something, reminding us of the holiness of God who when asked by Moses for an ID card and a name replied: 'I AM WHO I AM. . . . Tell the Israelites that I . . . have sent you to them' (Exodus 3.14–15). It is also a reminder of the question put by Jesus to the disciples at Caesarea Philippi: 'Who do people say that I am?' In other words: 'What is my identity?' The answer will soon be in a biometric ID card, the purpose of which is that your 'true' identity is known and is traceable. But identity actually means 'the state of being the same', deriving from the Latin *idem*, and identical means 'the exact same'. In fact identity means the unity of a thing within itself, its coherence, its lack of division or, in other words, its integrity. When we say that a person, or a church, or a nation, has integrity, surely this is what we mean. I am who I am.

For diversity to have integrity, it can neither mean endless separation of the parts of the body nor the dreaded uniformity. It does mean the consistency of a coherent identity in the love of God who is in Christ reconciling not just the church but the world and especially the poor, the forgotten and the despised. It means the riches of each person, being brought together

45

again, re-integrated, as an offering in reconciliation to God. It means bringing home the exiles, or the exiled parts of ourselves.

The most fundamental human integrity is that of spirit and body. The struggle to maintain that integrity, the wholeness of personhood, is acute. So much about our world tends toward disintegration. Political oppression and dispossession, extreme poverty, violence of every kind, racism, sexism, xenophobia, homophobia and the impoverishment of the imagination by consumer capitalism are all deeply damaging to bodies and spirits. Yet the worst threat comes, not from these things themselves, but from our internalization of them; the subtle ways in which they can colonize our inner landscape make us internalize their definition of who we are, incline us to live out of our fears and not our freedom.

The church has often colluded with this colonization, has fed our fears in the interest of its own power and forgotten that we are called to share in the glorious freedom of the children of God. The Canaanite woman, like Ruth, has not been colonized. In the face of insult and rejection, she refuses to accept this as the will of God, and confronts Jesus with her utter conviction that he can help her despite all their differences. She is who she is. And in that identity, she is confirmed.

Anointed into solidarity

And finally, in John 12, we find Mary of Bethany, another beloved disciple. She has been a supplicant before: when she desired to listen to Jesus teaching; when her brother died and she touched Jesus' heart with her weeping. But this time, we see Mary ministering to Jesus.

> From a high secret shelf, I take what I hid myself,
> Perfume precious and rare, never meant to spill or spare.
> This I'll carefully break, this I'll empty for his sake.
> I will give what I have to my Lord.[3]

Her anointing is an act of pure extravagance; Judas, protesting, tries to force an either/or division – either one can love Jesus or one can love the poor. But Jesus refutes Judas by affirming Mary's act. It is perfectly possible to love both; this is a false and ungenerous dichotomy.

This is a very personal story, yet its beauty and intimacy should not blind us to its wider significance. The story of the anointing anticipates three crucial scenes later in John's Gospel. First, Mary is anointing Jesus for a bitter and untimely death that both accept as the likely outcome of his challenge to the religious authority of Jerusalem. Jesus will be anointed again when he is laid in the tomb. At his death, Jesus will be anointed in secret by men who are afraid to make their faith public. Mary, however, anoints him in the presence of all who are dining with him. Her declaration for Jesus is not deferred until after his death but offered to him while he still lives. In so doing, she makes visible not just her love, but the violence to which Jesus is to be subjected. She is a model of resistance to violence through the love that acts.

Second, this anointing of Jesus' feet rather than his head anticipates the incident in John 13 when Jesus washes his disciples' feet. The footwashing models discipleship and service. But it is also, as the Gospel makes clear, a participation in Jesus' suffering and death. It is an act of service, but it is also a mark of identification in the events of Jesus' passion. Mary does for Jesus now what he will do for his disciples later.

Third, Mary's anointing anticipates the commandment that Jesus will give his followers. 'I give you a new commandment, that you love one another. Just as I have loved you, you also should love one another.' The depth of Mary's love for Jesus is signalled by the extravagance of her gift. In this story, Mary models what it means to be a disciple; to serve, to love one another, to share in Jesus' death and resurrection. It is an open invitation not just to talk about love, as Judas did, but to *be* the reminder, in our concrete decisions and actions, that if we have not love, we are nothing. Kosuke Koyama writes:

> What is love if it remains invisible and intangible? . . . Grace cannot function in a world of invisibility. Yet in our world, the rulers try to make invisible the alien, the orphan, the hungry and thirsty, the sick and imprisoned. This is violence. Their bodies must remain visible. There is a connection between invisibility and violence. People, because of the dignity of the image of God they embody, must remain seen. Faith, hope and love are not vital except in what is seen. Religion seems to raise up the invisible and despise what is visible. But it is the 'see, hear, touch' gospel that can nurture the hope which is free from deception.[4]

This is love, not as sentiment, but as a deep resistance to all that does violence to, demeans or degrades other human beings. It is also about receiving as well as giving. Jesus' acceptance of, and refusal to condemn, Mary's gift is also a gift of love. Finally, Jesus himself becomes the supplicant, giving dignity and grace to vulnerability and need. This is the way we are to be with one another, a way grounded firmly on mutual exchange, acceptance and respect for one another in all our difference, our frailty, our unexpressed and unmet need.

This is a very different notion of love to that which we have been socialized to accept. We live, for example, in a culture which has somehow come to accept a false connection between love and violence. Rather like the drunk sitting on a bar stool telling you how much he loves the children he hasn't been near for years. But love is not what you feel, love is what you do. To profess love and yet to do violence is to be tragically divided, disintegrated.

Our culture does not always understand or value the equal validity of many kinds of love, besotted as it is with somewhat infantile romantic fantasies. But the patient attentiveness of the carer, the mutual affection of friends, the deep bonds of brotherly and sisterly love, the companionship of many kinds of community and family life and the chosen solitude of the religious or artistic life all share that different way of seeing with the eyes of love. It is good that we should cherish them all.

Hard as it is for our society to value the servant role properly, when notions of public service have been demeaned, when every transaction is an economic one, it is even more difficult for us to allow ourselves to be served, especially when the service is a bodily one. It makes us vulnerable, exposes all our weaknesses. It turns us back into supplicants. But there is Jesus, kneeling at our feet.

> We cannot love our neighbours unless we are open to being loved by our neighbours. We cannot extend hospitality to strangers unless we accept hospitality from strangers. The gospel upholds this two-way traffic. One-way traffic breeds self-righteousness.[5]

The Scottish poet, Robert Burns, wrote, 'O, wad some power the giftie gie us, tae see oursels as ithers see us.'[6] And, 'Do for others what you would have them do for you,' said Jesus. This is two-way traffic; to see ourselves from the perspective of the other, and to extend to the other the same generosity and kindness that we wish to receive: 'Removing all traces of racism from our relations means affirming that we are different and that we shall remain different' (Edgard Pisani, former French Foreign Minister). Affirming the right of the 'not us' to be different is a huge responsibility, especially when we are in the majority, and have more choice in the matter; minorities often have to make do with the small space for expression of difference assigned to them. And this task is all the more challenging because we also have to discern what differences really *are* threatening and to resist all efforts to whip up hysteria about the rest. Our freedoms are not at risk in Europe. Our attachment to our own comforts is much more of a threat to our freedoms.

To see ourselves as others see us from the beach, not the terrace, is not comfortable. Racism depends on the dehumanization of the 'not us'. But it is also learned from the experience of racism. We must resist every effort to scapegoat and stigmatize, to divide into 'us' and 'them'. Racism makes 'human' the least important definition. The gospel makes it the most important.

Ruth was assimilated; the Canaanite woman was affirmed in her difference. These strategies we are familiar with in Europe. But Mary anointed Jesus into identification with the 'not us', the minority, the supplicants. I want to finish with another story. The minister in the church I visited in Guguletu, the Revd Spiwo Xapile, studied for a while in Scotland, and there heard a woman member of the Iona Community speak. She told of how, as a child in rural Scotland, some traveller children had come to her school. Travellers, who used to be known as gypsies, attract the same stigma and discrimination in Scotland as everywhere else. She described how she would stand at the school window, in tears at the sight of these children being bullied, taunted and pushed about. Then one day, she realized that it was not enough to weep. She had to leave her window, go over to where the traveller children were, and stand beside them. My South African friend had been very moved by this story – it had changed his understanding of his own ministry, and turned it into a quite remarkable and unusual one of service to and solidarity with people in his own very poor community living with HIV – another group who have experienced much discrimination and prejudice, not least from fellow Christians.

It was for me a vivid demonstration of the 'see, hear, touch' gospel, of the journey from assimilation through multiculturalism to solidarity with the poorest and most vulnerable which Jesus himself made, and invites us to make too. And it was a great example of how people taking on responsibility create ripples that cross boundaries, cross continents and bear witness to a different way of being.

5

The power of human dignity

'The glory of God is a human being fully alive'. So said St
Irenaeus, and made explicit the link between human dignity
and God's creativity. Christians affirm the good news of Jesus
Christ, that every person, every human community, the whole
creation, is created by God, wanted by God, loved by God.
Therefore, every person, and the earth that is their habitat, is of
infinite value. This value does not depend on the criteria the
world uses. We are unconditionally loved regardless of whether
we are useful, productive, beautiful, strong or successful.
Market forces do not set our value. We have intrinsic worth.
The word 'dignity' itself derives from the Latin *dignus*, meaning
'worth'. Jesus embodied the potential of life lived in solidarity
with the initiatives of God. He was fully alive. All that degrades
or denies that potential is a kind of blasphemy, all that cher-
ishes and affirms it is praise.

It is an outstanding characteristic of Jesus' person and ministry that he reached out again and again to the people whom
the world excluded or counted as valueless, and included
them in the human community, the inclusive community of
God's love, not just fishermen but women, foreigners, prosti-
tutes, thieves and publicans, the sick, the mentally deranged,
the poorest of the poor. He held them up as being closer to
God's reality than the self-righteous, the justified and the
respectable.

Always in human societies there has been the destructive
urge to limit who is human, to compare and exclude. Black
lives have been considered less fully human than white lives,

female lives less than male, Muslim lives less than Christian, Jewish lives less than Gentile, Palestinian lives less than Israeli, homosexual lives less than heterosexual. And always, including today, the lives of poor, strange or marginalized people have been considered less fully human, less precious, more expendable than the lives of rich people.

Let me recall a story from the Hebrew Bible of a young woman trafficked to a foreign country as a domestic servant; used as a surrogate mother by a wealthy woman desperate because her female identity, security and honour depended on bearing children, then cast off and abandoned with her child to die in a wilderness. It is the story of Hagar.

This is a woman without a land, uprooted, removed from all that her land could offer her – the means of providing for her child, a place to belong, people to belong with. Like trafficked and enslaved people everywhere, her rights were taken away from her. Even the territory of her body was invaded, colonized, plundered – and then abandoned, dumped in no man's land.

It would be a travesty of justice to read this story as just an incident, however regrettable, in someone's personal religious drama. It's a political story too. Of course, it predates the jubilee teaching of Leviticus 25, of restoration of land, freedom from slavery and the cancellation of debts. But even the ideal of jubilee was unthinkable for Hagar. For her, there was only the desolation of landlessness, powerlessness and the fear of watching her child die.

But we also hear that God heard Hagar crying, and God's angel spoke to her – words of comfort, words of promise. Promise of survival first, but then that great promise that resounds through the whole of the Hebrew Bible – 'You will become a nation.' It is a promise to the Jews – but not just to the Jews, also to the Egyptian Hagar: 'You will become a nation.' They were communal times; there was no thought of liberation, of hope for the future outside that promise. 'You will become a nation' could equally be said of the landless of the world today – and a great nation it is, to be sure.

In the New Testament, the promise has a different emphasis. Here, the nation is not one based on blood or kinship. There is no Promised Land. In Paul's exegesis of the story of Sarah and Hagar, the promise is one of freedom and a different kind of deliverance, into the community of justice and love. Whatever the dispensation of the individual, justice and love are never individual, private matters. They are only possible in the context of the community. This is the meaning of the nation.

The nation of women

The story of Hagar is a comment on the nation of the landless; but even more, it is a sobering reflection on how little has changed for so many of the nation of women.

During the 1990s, the nation of women gained some prominence on the global stage through a number of worldwide movements, in particular, the agenda that emerged from the UN Decade for Women, and its global consultation in Beijing. This was paralleled in Christian churches by the World Council of Churches' Ecumenical Decade of Churches in Solidarity with Women. This agenda identified four key concerns that showed remarkable consistency, whether the women were coming from poor southern countries or rich northern ones. These four concerns, which were seen as closely interrelated, were:

- *The invisibility of women*; their low level of access to and participation in structures of both society and church; in leadership, in decision-making, in availability of resources, education and information.
- *Racism and xenophobia*, which are emerging in new forms across the world: in ethnic cleansing, in the increased numbers of refugees and asylum-seekers; in internal ethnic and racial conflicts, as well as in their more wearily familiar guises.

- *Economic injustice*; the adverse impact of globalized economic systems affects women and children disproportionately.
- And last, but by no means least, *violence against women*.

Of course, these four are not only women's concerns. But they are overwhelmingly the most important ones, raised again and again from Canada to Cameroon, and from Nottingham to Nairobi. Furthermore, they unite women of different faiths and none. They do not affect only women, and it would be ludicrous to suggest that. But beyond question, they affect more women, more acutely and with more profound consequences. Remember that famous UN statistic: *women make up half the world's population, do two-thirds of the world's productive work, own 10 per cent of the world's wealth and 1 per cent of the world's land.* Women are still hugely disempowered and the more powerless you are, the easier it is for power to be wielded against you. This is particularly true with regard to sexual health; in many places, women have no power to negotiate sexual activity. This makes them especially at risk of contracting HIV, and then of being anathematized when they do. Added to the onerous responsibility of being the harder-working sex, women suffer more because of their role as primary carers. And their low profile in decision-making means that the kind of policies that would be family-friendly for women and their dependants often take second place to other interests; whether these be the interests of corporate shareholders, the military industrial complex or powerful local elites.

The story of Hagar comes from a time long ago. But it still illustrates a global reality. In a globalized world, the violence of poverty that is a denial of human rights may affect 95 per cent of women in one country and only 20 per cent in another. In one country, poverty may mean extreme destitution, even starvation, and death at 30. In another, it may mean eking out an existence of social exclusion on the margins of an affluent society and having a life expectancy of 15 years less than the woman in the leafy suburb next door. But the causes of their poverty will be the same. They are redundant to the requirements of a globalized free-market economy.

The story of Hagar is one of profound gender and sexual violence, from a scripture full of such stories. Violence against women today takes many forms: domestic abuse, incest and child sexual abuse, sexual harassment, rape and sexual violence, unrealistic and degrading representations of women in the media, trafficking in women (a modern form of slavery), institutional gender violence, gender violence in war – and this is by no means an exhaustive list. And for women already invisible, economically oppressed and subject to violence, racism and xenophobia compound every threat.

Christian Aid, the Make Poverty History alliance, the Trade Justice movement, G8 campaigning, all focus on overcoming global poverty. Their central aims – trade justice, debt cancellation, increased and appropriate aid – are primarily economic, but they also affect, and inevitably have to take into consideration, the other components that have accelerated the feminization of poverty – the invisibility of women, violence against women and racism and xenophobia.

That the recognition, affirmation and support of the human dignity of women is a crucial factor, perhaps *the* crucial factor in a sustainable future for life on earth, is emphasized by the fact that two of the eight Millennium Development Goals are directly concerned with female health and well-being.

The Millennium Development Goals were adopted by the UN in 2000, and signed up to by 189 countries. They are:

- Eradicate extreme poverty and hunger.
- Achieve universal primary education.
- Promote gender equality and empower women.
- Reduce child mortality.
- Improve maternal health.
- Combat HIV/AIDS, malaria and other diseases.

- Ensure environmental sustainability.
- Develop a global partnership for development.

Of course, these goals are about more than just the interests and well-being of women. But their achievement would benefit women disproportionately, precisely because women suffer their absence disproportionately. All of them are about increasing security – of habitat, of livelihood, of health and education – all of which reduce the likelihood of war and conflict. They are also about creating sustainable communities, and they recognize the importance of women in that process to the extent that the empowerment of women is an explicit goal. It is increasingly recognized that global, sustainable development depends on women. That's not just because they do so much of the productive work. It's also because women are the primary carers, and the transmitters of knowledge through the generations and through communities, particularly with regard to health and education. But the capacity this represents will not be properly utilized without women's political, cultural and economic empowerment.

Goals 3 and 5 relate directly to women. But all of the others will either rely on or equally include women if they are to be successful. For the power of intrinsic human dignity manifested by women in the most difficult, oppressive and intransigent circumstances is a timely reminder that, although relentlessly victimized, women are also, and predominantly, strong, capable and responsible survivors. They are workers, farmers, creators and cultivators. They are caregivers to children, the very old, the dependent ill and infirm, the excluded and impoverished, and of course, to men. They are caretakers of families, communities, of the built environment and of the earth itself. They are peacemakers, mediators, educators and the bedrock of civil society. Personal, communal and human well-being and sustainability are not possible without the empowerment of women and the proper valuing of their human dignity.

This empowerment can only take place in the nation of justice and love, which is to be found in the followers of all religions and none, among all who affirm the power of non-selective and unconditional human dignity. This nation of justice and love would seem to be the only community in which the desperate questions of land, peace, trade, indebtedness, aid, health, education and development can be negotiated without endless rounds of dispossession, slaughter, hunger, disease and despair.

It's easy to be cynical about such a community. But the nation of people across the world who want to be part of the community of justice and love may be bigger than we think. The overwhelming public response to the Asian tsunami in 2004 suggests so. The struggle is more one of how to effect change in the face of unaccountable institutions. Which takes us back to politics, and the need to strategize in ways that mobilize the nation of justice and love beyond the limitations of the nation state, or any particular religion or ideology – surely an ecumenical task for the great nation we represent beyond our individual nations.

In the words of Musimbi Kanyoro, women know that

> during his life here on earth, Jesus visited the towns and villages and saw with his own eyes the problems facing the people. He saw the poverty, the inequality, the religious and economic oppression, the unemployment, the depression, the physically ill and the socially unclean. His heart was filled with pity. He pronounced what his mission was all about: he came to preach the good news to the poor and to release those who are captives and give health to those who are ill.[1]

In him, they see the possibility of a true community of women and men.

In searching for hints of that true community, women all over the world have been reading the Bible and the history of the church from another angle, rediscovering the hidden histories, the silenced voices, the notes in the margins. They are seeking the women and men whose spirituality is one of hope, persistence, courage and compassion. They are drinking from the wells being uncovered in many places, in many traditions, in the wisdom of the body and the wisdom of the earth.

For the sake of that future, therefore, and the vision of the nation of justice and love, people of goodwill everywhere will need to show solidarity and to be held accountable for being part of change and transformation.

If we believe that women love human dignity, support it with their energy, time, talents and unfailing work across the world, and if we value that love and ability, then we must be accountable for working to ensure that women are included, informed and represented at all levels in decision-making and leadership in our institutions. We must take on the burdens of responsibility and the risks of speaking out in public.

If we believe, with practically every public health body in the world, that the best way of improving the health and well-being of the whole community is by educating women, and if we value the health of communities, then we must be accountable for working to ensure that education for girls and women is given as high a priority as the education of boys and men. We must strive to create a culture in which learning is not despised as unmanly.

If we believe that our belonging in the human community is a family loyalty above all others, and that the wound of the daughter of our sister or brother's people wounds us too, then we must be accountable for working for the reform of racist immigration laws, and for safeguarding the human dignity of refugees and asylum-seekers.

If we believe that all people have intrinsic human dignity, and that that dignity is denied every time violence is perpetrated on women and children and on men who do not conform to dominant images of masculinity, then we must be accountable for refusing any ideology that legitimizes gender violence, and for breaking the silence and complicity with violence of our institutions. Men must begin to take responsibility for male violence, refusing to see it as a 'woman's problem' or expecting women to solve it for men. And women will recognize and affirm the solidarity demonstrated by considerable numbers of men, and work for a diversity of human community in which women and men are valued equally.

Women of dignity

I want to share some stories of women who exemplify for me the power of human dignity. In 1998, I attended the Women's Festival held at the General Assembly of the World Council of Churches in Harare, Zimbabwe. While I was there, I met a French-speaking Methodist deaconess, Marie-Thérèse. She came from the Democratic Republic of the Congo, a huge country in which all the problems that beset Africa are present to a desperate degree. It is the scene of a bloody and rumbling war, complicated not only by warring factions but by the undisciplined forces of half a dozen other African countries, which breaks into open conflict regularly, and where low-grade hostilities are a normal way of life. It has enormous numbers of refugees and displaced peoples. HIV/AIDS is a huge problem. And, though it is a beautiful country rich in natural resources, the combination of asset-stripping, war and chaos has left the people tremendously impoverished.

On the last day, I went to see Marie-Thérèse off on her journey home. She was there with a group of other women from the Congo, all of them involved in church and community projects in their towns and villages – caring for people with HIV/AIDS, for refugees and war victims, for some of the many orphans created by the tragedies of their country, for women struggling to support big families with few resources. They had travelled to Zimbabwe by a rickety bus that looked as if it wouldn't get to the end of the street, never mind back to the Congo. When it started up, it made terrible noises and belched fumes. These women were going to spend three days and nights on this bus, driving through some of the most dangerous parts of Africa, sleeping and eating on the bus. It was a profoundly humbling experience to meet these women; I could hardly imagine the struggles and difficulties they faced. And yet, the astonishing thing about them was how joyful, how full of laughter and hope they were.

I asked them why they had made this long, uncomfortable and dangerous journey to East Africa. 'It's so important for us to have this chance to meet Christian women from other parts of the world,' they replied. 'It's an encouragement for us; we feel we are not alone. We want to learn about the problems women face in other places, and to share faith with them.' I think they had found that encouragement; I certainly know I had found it in them.

Another friend of mine in Scotland recently took a very long walk. She walked the West Highland Way (a 95-mile rural trail) in the company of a number of young people from the poorest parts of Glasgow. They weren't young people who were used to outdoor pursuits, so they had to do a lot of training in the gym and on practice walks to get fit enough for their expedition, and my friend gave up her spare time to do it with them. They had to raise money for proper equipment. She's someone you couldn't blame for sitting back and enjoying what leisure time she has – she has a single parent who had experienced considerable personal tragedy in her life, and has survived what would stop most of us in our tracks. But she's chosen instead to try to give something positive and creative to young people who have very little positive and creative in their lives. She too dares to care.

Volunteering in an HIV programme in Kenya, my daughter met Jayne Mutahi, who runs Hands of Compassion, an outreach project. Jayne has, in the past four years, accumulated

nine tents and a second-hand vehicle and made it her objective
to take HIV-testing and medical treatment to the Masai tribe,
who often live as far as ten hours from any health care. The
Masai are a popular attraction with western tourists visiting
Kenya but their numbers are declining. They have continued
to practise their ancient rituals and ceremonies, choosing a
peaceful way of life that is centred on rearing their cattle, but
their polygamous practices accelerate the spread of HIV
throughout families.

Jayne relies on intermittent sponsorship and donations from
friends and volunteers to carry out the mobile clinics. On a
typical four-day clinic, over three hundred people are assessed
and given treatment by the nurses and a hundred are tested for
HIV. Everyone who comes for treatment or testing is given food
and water and there is daily worship in English, Masai and
Swahili, so that a strong sense of unity and friendship develops
between the many different tribes and cultures involved with
the project. The clinics are the only link the people have to
information about health issues, family planning or HIV, and
they mean a great deal to them.

Kosuke Koyama challenges us:

> What is love if it remains invisible and intangible? Those
> who do not love a brother or sister whom they have seen
> cannot love God whom they have not seen. The devastat-
> ing poverty in which millions of children live is visible.
> Racism is visible. Machine guns are visible. Slums are vis-
> ible. The gap between rich and poor is glaringly visible.
> Our response to these realities must be visible . . . It is the
> 'see, hear, touch' gospel that can nurture the hope which
> is free from deception.[2]

There are three things I notice about people who get involved
in these ways. The first is that they are always *practical*; they are
about making changes through what people can do together.
The second is that they are always *learning*. Through becoming

involved, they also learn a considerable amount about the people and places they are seeking to support. Care is always most meaningful when it is informed – and this is a virtuous circle, because learning enriches both those who are being supported, and also those who are doing the supporting. And the third thing that I notice is that this kind of working and learning together builds *community*. It involves an investment of time and money; it also involves a lot of laughter and creativity. It gives value to the people who are being supported. But it also gives value to the people working together in this way. It is the 'see, hear, touch' gospel in action.

This involvement reflects a real solidarity with those who, as Koyama says, the powerful try to make invisible, those people who live on the margins.

The God who runs out to the margins

Jesus told a story which begins, 'Once upon a time, there was a man who had two sons . . .' I love this story; it seems to me to contain all that is at the heart of Jesus. You remember how the younger son claimed his share of the inheritance, went to a country far away, and squandered it all on riotous living. This story happens often, with only minor differences of detail. The country he was living in also fell on hard times; the young man was at his wits' end, homeless and cold and penniless; eventually he was so hungry that he even considered eating the pig feed at the farm he was working on because no one else would give him anything to eat. Lonely and desperate, and most of all humiliated that he'd got himself into this terrible state, he thought about the home that he'd left, where everyone had plenty, and he came to a big decision. He turned and started for home.

When the young man was still quite a long way off, his father saw him coming, and when he saw how thin and miserable he looked, his heart was filled with love and concern. He stopped what he was doing, and he *ran* out to meet him. He threw his arms round him and kissed him. The young man tried to apologize, but his father wasn't really listening to his apology. He was too busy seeing what his son needed, calling people to go and get the best robe, and shoes and a ring for his finger, and to prepare a feast. Go quickly. Now!

This is an extraordinary story. It is all about a God who runs out to the margins to meet us, and who is too busy taking care of us to be bothered with our apologies and excuses. You were not here, and now you are. That's all that matters. Let me see what you need. Let's celebrate. Jesus was always telling us this story in one form or another. Remember the one about the messenger who was sent to bring everyone to the great feast, and how those who accepted the invitation were the ones on the margins, on the periphery of society. Care is to lay the table, quickly, now.

But Jesus didn't just tell the story. He lived it too. Jesus becomes the face of God running out to find us. He went out to ordinary people close by – to children and fishermen, civil servants and grandmothers and shopkeepers. But he didn't stop there. He went out to people who drank too much, people who never went to the temple, and those the respectable disapproved of. But he didn't stop there. He went out to asylum-seekers, foreigners and the people everyone was scared of. He went out to criminals and people in prison. But he didn't even stop there. He went to the place where people get arrested, tortured and killed. And he got killed too. He went so there would be no one, anywhere, who was too far away, and all the time he was saying, 'Yes. You. You too!'

In going out, we find that we are not alone. People don't just sit passively, waiting for someone to show up and take care of them. All the work that goes on to overcome marginalization happens because there are already people there, taking the risks of caring. Wherever people are living on the knife-edge, they are trying to overcome poverty, to offer family support, to help survivors of violence of one kind or another. On the margins of power, such people abound.

In spite of everything, care persists. The urge and desire to care are still enormously strong. Whether in supporting large national organizations like Christian Aid or small local movements and groups, people are entering into new relationships, new partnerships. This is tremendously important. Many of these projects are small and struggling. They are not glamorous or vote-catching. Sometimes they are almost invisible. They need and deserve our support. But this is more than a one-way traffic. It is also a conversation, a dialogue.

> From you I receive, to you I give
> Together we share, and from this we live.[3]

6

Living hopefully

In the Sermon on the Mount, Jesus reminds his listeners that God makes the rain to fall on the just and the unjust alike. That phrase always fascinated me as a child, growing up in Scotland, where the combination of a cold, damp climate and Presbyterian cultural pessimism meant that rain was experienced as a curse. Anyone who has ever stood day after day waiting for a bus as a bitter wind whips in off the North Sea or the Atlantic, driving a soaking, miserable drizzle before it, will know what I mean. It was not until I visited hot, dusty, water-parched Israel that I realized that rain there comes as the bringer of new life and growth, as sweetness and refreshment and delightful coolness. There, it comes as blessing. It puts a very different perspective on the rain falling on the just and unjust alike.

That experience taught me two things. The first was that the Bible always has to be read in context. The second was that you have to be pretty careful when dealing with the weather in the Bible. The theologian Jürgen Moltmann identifies a tendency among Christians to concentrate on the text they preach rather than the context in which the gospel must be proclaimed, and context is pretty crucial when you're trying to track a hurricane, or read the sky.

Genesis 9 describes the covenant God made with Noah in the aftermath of the flood. And the sign of that covenant is the rainbow. Whenever the sky is covered with clouds, and the rainbow appears, Noah is told, that will be a reminder not only to Noah, but also to God, of the promise God has made. A God who needs an aide-memoire is an appealing thought; a God who chooses a rainbow is quite delightful.

A rainbow is still a powerful sign; though not perhaps in the same context. Small children put it in their paintings because of its *beauty* and *unexpectedness*; it emerges from behind dark clouds and says, 'I beg to differ'. For millions of people, its different colours, flowing into one another so you can't really tell where one stops and the other starts, are a symbol of *diversity and inclusion*. Sometimes that is as a sign of welcome to the diversity of sexuality of those who fly a rainbow banner, or the diversity of the rainbow nation, South Africa, or the political diversity of reds and greens and purples and pinks. In different contexts, the rainbow has different meanings. I don't know how many of these different contexts would think of it as a sign of covenant. But for all of them, it's a sign of *hope*, a promise that somewhere behind the dark clouds, the sun is shining. And without hope, the Bible says, the people perish.

But let's go back to the covenant. It is God's promise that never again will a flood destroy the whole earth. Now quite the most remarkable thing about this covenant is the fact that God does not just make it with human beings. It is made with all living beings. Only once does the text address Noah and his descendants. But six times, God makes a covenant with all living beings. Hubris, the pride that puts humankind at the apex of the triangle, is given short shrift here.

In the late Middle Ages, the poets of Scotland were known as 'Makars', makers. In Genesis 2, we find a wonderful picture of God the Makar. There is something rather touching, both literally and emotionally, about this God, so profoundly human in his activity – modelling a man out of the earth's clay, animating (literally, breathing life into) him, then planting a beautiful garden full of magical trees and treasure for him to live in. But the man himself is as much a part of the earth as all the other forms and species. His very name, Adam, links him with the ground (*Adamah*) of his being. He is created, not creator.

The failure to acknowledge creatureliness has been a big problem for human beings ever since – and an ever bigger one for the other life forms we share the earth with. Our tendency to assume that the universe is at our disposal, that it has no intrinsic worth other than its utility to the human species has made us careless to the point of extreme culpability. In the last twenty-five years alone, we have destroyed *30 per cent* of our non-renewable natural environment. It is a kind of blasphemy.

The search for our ancestors is greatly in vogue at present, and there's plenty of that in the Bible too. It's a fascinating subject, but really not as important as how *our* descendants, our children's grandchildren, will look back at us. What will we pass on to them? How will they judge us?

To be creature, not creator, one among many living species, is to come face to face with our limitations. We are not God, and God is not just an idealized version of us. God is other, and speaks to us in other voices. Our judgement of the world, sometimes expressed as if we had a monopoly on divine truth, is in truth that which holds us most to account. In Micah 6 (verses 1–2), the prophet calls the people as if to a court of law to listen to what God is saying, and this is what God the plaintiff says:

> Arise, plead your case before the mountains,
>   and let the hills hear your voice.
> Hear, you mountains, the controversy of the LORD,
>   and you enduring foundations of the earth;
>   for the LORD has a controversy with his people,
>   and he will contend with Israel.

There can be no clearer indication anywhere in scripture that to be a creature in the covenant is not only to be required to be in right relationship with our own human kind, but with the whole creation. Justice is also eco-justice. And how, then, will the mountains judge us? Will the enduring foundations of the earth find in our favour? Nowhere are these questions more crucial than in relation to climate change.

What is climate change?

Climate change, global warming, the greenhouse effect, all describe a process by which the activities of people are disrupting the global systems which control the climate. The earth's atmosphere acts like a greenhouse – the gases in the atmosphere insulate the earth so that some of the sun's heat is retained. The temperature at the earth's surface affects a wide range of ecological systems and cycles, including the climate, the water cycle and the oceans. The temperature at the earth's surface is increasing due to our use of fossil fuels.

In the past two hundred years or so, human activity has depended increasingly on energy derived from fossil fuels – coal, gas and oil. Fossil fuels are the fossilized remains of plants which were alive 300 million years ago. When energy is released from fossil fuels, usually by burning them in power stations and motor engines, carbon dioxide (CO_2) is released. It is the increasing amount of carbon dioxide being put into the atmosphere that is the main cause behind global warming.

The main impacts of global warming are a rise in the level of the ocean as the ice caps melt and a disruption in the climate: changing patterns of weather, a greater frequency of floods, droughts and violent storms. As sea levels rise, coastal floods and erosion increase and low-lying land will become submerged. Some islands are expected to completely disappear. There are also likely to be biological changes, as the ranges of some species expand and others contract. Some pest species are expected to become more common, while some rare species may become extinct.

Because it is so complex, it is not possible to forecast exactly what will happen but the trends are predictable and are already in evidence. Six of the ten warmest years on record were in the 1990s. The Arctic ice is shrinking each year by an area the size of the Netherlands. By 2050, it is expected that 1 in 12 properties in Scotland will be at risk from flooding.

CO_2 emissions in the UK amount to ten tonnes per person per year. To get this into perspective, if global CO_2 emissions were kept at levels that could be safely absorbed by the earth's cycles, the average would amount to a little over one tonne per person per year. In other words, we in the UK are currently using ten times our fair share of the atmosphere to dump the CO_2 spent in maintaining our lifestyle. The victims of this commandeering of a greater share of the atmosphere are not only those who are exposed to the floods, droughts and hurricanes. They are also the poorest countries (India emits 1.2 tonnes per person per year; Haiti emits 0.2) and future generations, who will be left a less habitable world.

The biggest culprit is the USA, which with 4 per cent of the world's population, uses 25 per cent of the world's oil and emits 20 tonnes of CO_2 per person annually. Research has calculated the cost of the carbon debt generated by the emissions of the rich countries, and it is estimated to come to US$1 trillion dollars annually.[1] That is the scale by which the rich countries' economies are being subsidized by the earth and its peoples.

At the current rate of carbon emissions, global average temperatures will rise 2° C by 2050 according to research by the Intergovernmental Panel on Climate Change. Most experts agree that this increase is already signed, sealed and ready for delivery. Expected consequences include:

- The creation of 150 million environmental refugees – overwhelmingly in poor countries.
- Acute water shortages for 1–3 billion people.
- 30 million more people going hungry as agricultural yields go into recession across the globe.

- Sea levels edging towards increases of up to 95 cm by the end of the century, submerging 18 per cent of Bangladesh.

Not that we have to wait until then for the problems to start.

- A 1° C rise, expected by 2020, would see an extra 240 million people experiencing water 'stress' – where supply can no longer be stretched to meet demand.
- The predicted 1.3° C rise by 2025 would see tens of millions more going hungry due to falling agricultural yields in the developing world and rising global food prices.[2]

Reading the signs of the times

Jesus talked about the weather too. In our contemporary context, his words are pretty direct. He said, don't pretend you don't know how to read the signs. And threw the challenge back to his listeners; you know what needs to be done, why don't you do it?

At the heart of the Christian gospel is an identification with all living beings, and a demonstration of a different way of transcending limits, not by rolling over them, but by embracing and transforming them. Jesus did not voluntarily seek out suffering, and did not glorify it, but he chose to bear it rather than inflict it on others. The sign of the bread and wine on the communion table are a reminder to us, a bit like the rainbow is for God, that apart from all living beings we have no life, that we are creature not creator, and that what is given, and given up, in love, is never lost or wasted.

So what might it mean to live hopefully, casting our lot with those who age after age, with no extraordinary power, reconstitute the world? Koyama says that 'the gospel insists on visibility – the emaciated bodies of starved children must remain visible. There is a connection between invisibility and violence.'[3]

Making things visible

This connection between invisibility and violence is particularly strongly evidenced in war: I think of the refusal of the 'coalition of the willing' to count the Iraqi dead, of the secrecy around Guantànamo Bay, around extraordinary rendition. But it's also a part of much ecological destruction. Who in the West really knows what is going on in the Niger delta, in Bolivia, in Bangladesh? They merit a couple of lines in the broadsheets, or a bit more if a celebrity takes an interest in them. Come to that, who knows what's going on with asbestos-poisoned workers in Dumbartonshire, or around toxic dumps in North Lanark? *To live hopefully means making the violence done to people and places visible*; to say what we have seen, to ask what is still unseen, to break the culture of silence and to name names.

There are, of course, many ways to do this: through campaigns and lobbying and letter-writing and all the things organizations like Christian Aid have years of experience of doing. Sometimes it is simply to draw attention by presence. When members of the Iona Community sit down outside Faslane Nuclear Base, we do not think that blockading is going to close the base then and there. We do it to make visible once again the huge capacity for death and destruction contained in every Trident submarine. It is what the Ecumenical Accompaniment Programme in Palestine and Israel (EAPPI), a programme run by Quaker Peace and Social Witness, does in the West Bank and Jerusalem. (Christian Aid supports EAPPI, an initiative of the World Council of Churches.) In other places such as Iraq and Guatemala, teams of peace and solidarity activists make visible, often at high personal cost, the violence done to people and places that is not counted.

But bearing witness is about more than just making violence visible. It is also about *making alternatives visible*. Camas is the Iona Community's outdoor centre on the Ross of Mull, near the Iona ferry. Two miles off the road, just getting there is an adventure. Supplies have to be carried, or brought in by boat. Electricity for heating water comes from solar panels and a windmill; light comes from oil lamps, sunshine and stars; heat from wood stoves. Once you arrive at this remote fishing station, set in old quarry cottages on a beautiful little bay, there's plenty more adventure to be had: kayaking, abseiling, camping out overnight in caves, exploring the rugged landscape of the Ross of Mull. We've developed an organic garden and native species woodland. Camas is a great resource for young people, schools and people with special needs, especially those experiencing poverty or disadvantage.

When the Iona Community went on pilgrimage to Camas a couple of years ago, they were asked by the Camas staff as they were leaving to pick up a piece of rubbish from the large pile lying at the foot of the track, and carry it up to the road end. From there, some would be collected by Argyll and Bute Council refuse lorries. Some would go elsewhere for recycling. Some might be carried away by passers-by who could see a useful function for it. This request was not just a symbolic gesture. It was a pertinent reminder that everything that gets taken down the track to Camas has to be disposed of in some way. Everything that is not used or consumed has to be shipped or carried out, in the same way that it came in!

Having to assume personal responsibility for the waste we create makes us think differently about it. If you have to carry every tin can and plastic bag for two miles, you try to minimize that burden. You reduce what you buy; you reuse everything you can in the house or garden; you recycle as much as possible of what's left. You try to ensure that what you buy has the minimum of packaging. You begin to ask questions about what you really need, as opposed to what you just think you want. You begin to think differently about rubbish, especially when you are surrounded by such beauty. There's nothing as effective as finding a sanitary towel or an empty crisp packet on the beach to make you aware of the real nature of pollution. This assumption of personal responsibility even extends to human waste products, which are utilized as compost for the new trees. Waste management becomes a concern of the whole community, rather than something out of sight and out of mind.

Increasingly, waste management will be more difficult to keep out of sight and mind. Fly-tipping costs Scotland alone £11 million annually to deal with. But that's only the tip of the iceberg. A recent survey showed that one-sixth of British food budgets goes on the cost of packaging alone. And about *17 billion* plastic bags are handed out by the nine main supermarket companies, enough to cover all of Sussex and Surrey. If we continue at our present rate, the whole of England could be covered in plastic bags in just over twenty years! If that seems fanciful, or simply a problem of affluence, anyone who has travelled in poor countries will have seen how the accumulation of rubbish can kill livestock, poison and choke terrain and water, and blight whole landscapes.

Only a quarter of what we pay for our food is actually for the food. The rest goes on packaging, processing, transport, overheads, advertising and supermarket markups. All of these in their turn create waste products which require to be disposed of somewhere and somehow. There is a mania of consumption here producing a mountain of waste which uses up precious natural resources (seven supermarket chains have lorry mileage of 408 million miles a year), pollutes our environment and which we do not take adequate responsibility for disposing of. We seem increasingly unable to distinguish between what we need and what we want, and this inability may, in the end, kill us.

Waste management and responsibility is a part of everyday life at Camas. But it's only a start. Developing the organic garden, both to produce more of our food and to be a means of allowing urban young people to learn about and participate in caring for the environment; securing and maintaining the buildings in ways which are consistent with sustainability, simplicity and responsible energy use; all of these are ways in which the

Community is seeking to practise what we preach. But above all, Camas is a place in which it is possible to reflect on, and begin to heal, the disordered relationship between our needs and our wants. Food and shelter for everyone, community and acceptance, work that contributes to the well-being of everyone, safety and adventure, opportunities for creativity and beauty, tears, laughter, silence and song and the invitation to grow in relationship with our habitat, with one another, with our own deepest selves, with God – these are the needs we seek to meet.

The Iona Community, from a tradition which holds to the sacramental character of the whole creation, does not make distinctions between the sacred and the secular, but believes in the active self-communication of God in and through the things of this world. The ninth-century Irish theologian, John Scotus Eriugena, said: 'Every visible and invisible creature can be called a theophany, an appearance of the divine.' And the Christian Celts of Scotland used to refer to God's little book, the Bible, and God's great book, the creation, and read God in both. People who would resist reading the Bible readily read the creation at Camas. We offer people a space to do that. Remarkably often, people draw the conclusion that the creation is something to be grateful for, to be respectful of, and to cherish.

Interestingly, Camas is a place where the Bible can come alive. Many of its stories, particularly in the Gospels, depend on the experience of closeness to the elements and subsistence upon it. This experience is still, of course, that of much of the world's population today. In our urban, comfortable life, this is mediated to us, we are told about it. At Camas, it is immediate. We depend on the elements – light, water, wind, fire, soil – and we participate directly in them for our subsistence, through growing vegetables, baking bread, cutting wood and peat, and sailing boats and needing to know about weather, tides and phases of the moon.

Camas is a place where people are required to live in the 'here' (this place) and 'now' (this moment). They don't have to be defined by either a damaged past or a possible dismal future. They are accepted in the here and now. It's also a place where bodies matter. Working together at Camas, we have to feed and shelter our bodies and deal with bodily waste. It communicates the message that bodies matter, that they are holy, whether it is the human body, the bodies of other creatures or the earth body itself. This life in the present, and this holiness, is incarnational.

Camas is a place of significant change and new possibility for many people. The experience of creation and incarnation in new forms that challenge received messages is a liberating one. It is a kind of transformation. It gives people a new way of looking at what really matters, and challenges the hegemony of possessions, status, celebrity, appearance, luxury, power, violence, sectarianism, racism and all the other idols of our society. These three aspects of creation, incarnation and transformation connect in a dynamic relationship which is expressed in and through community.

For the Iona Community, this is a vital part of what it means to be part of the community of justice and love. We cannot be concerned about global poverty or indeed about poverty in Britain without also being concerned about environmental justice and ecological responsibility. The rich countries of the world are using up far, far more than their fair share of the earth's resources. It is a kind of theft, not just of the resources of poor countries but of their future. But it's our future too. We are all in this together, and finally we are beginning to understand that our very survival is tied up with theirs. We are indeed part of a single body in which, 'if one part suffers, all the other parts suffer with it' (1 Corinthians 12.26).

Some years ago, Jonathon Porritt, searching for the reasons why people do not take ecological issues seriously enough, said:

Simply, not enough people are dying yet in our countries; of skin cancer, of UV rays, or from pollution toxification illnesses. Nor are enough coastal communities drowning yet from rising sea-levels due to global warming. The visible, tangible, avoidable consequences of eco-disaster are not yet powerful enough to persuade sufficient people to change today's priorities.[4]

But that was before Hurricane Katrina, before flooding across England. We all have to take climate change seriously now.

That is why the Iona Community is committed to the Christian Aid Cut the Carbon Campaign, and to working to cut our carbon emissions by 5 per cent year on year. None of us thinks this will be easy. It will require major change and giving up much that we presently take for granted. But as we have learned at Camas, learning to differentiate between our wants and our needs is not all doom and gloom. We have more resources for transformation than we might think.

What we do at Camas and in the rest of our life and work is small. But that doesn't make it insignificant. We do what we can, not what we can't. We mourn what has been destroyed; we regret all that we cannot do. But we do not let it paralyse us. For we are also a community of resurrection. So we choose to live hopefully.

7

The journey is long

Oh Mary, don't you weep, don't you mourn
Oh Mary, don't you weep, don't you mourn
Pharaoh's army got drowned
Oh Mary, don't you weep.

If I could, I surely would
Stand on the rock where Moses stood.
Pharaoh's army got drowned
Oh Mary, don't you weep.
                    (African-American spiritual)

The Civil Rights Movement

I first heard 'Oh Mary, don't you weep' as a child on Iona in the early 1960s. It's an African-American spiritual, and became an important anthem for the Civil Rights Movement in America during that decade. It was often sung at ceilidhs and in worship on Iona, along with other songs from the struggle to end the political, economic and social apartheid that existed in the southern states of the USA. There, it was called segregation, but it was the same thing; a brutal and discriminatory system, sanctioned by the state and held in place by the racist attitudes of the majority white population. Slavery might have ended after the American Civil War, but its legacy lived on. Desegregating schools, restaurants, civic amenities and public transport were important parts of the struggle – so was registering black people to the vote that they were, in theory, eligible for, but who experienced acute hostility and violence when they attempted to exercise that right.

The Civil Rights Movement was deeply rooted in Christianity. The religious aspect of the movement was clearly evident in its songs, many of which were spirituals that came from the time of slavery, and took as their defining narrative and model the Exodus, the deliverance of the people of Israel out of slavery in Egypt.

'If I could, I surely would stand on the rock where Moses stood', refers to a passage in the book of Exodus (chapter 17) when the Israelites were wandering in the wilderness with no water to drink. They began to complain to Moses: why did you bring us out of Egypt just to die of thirst? The Bible says that Moses prayed earnestly and the Lord told him to strike a rock at Mount Sinai with his stick. So Moses did that, and the sweet water gushed out. The Bible also says that the place was named Massah, which means 'testing', and Meribah, which means 'complaining', because it was here that the Israelites complained, and put the Lord to the test by asking, 'Is the Lord with us or not?' The water from the rock didn't only save their lives; it became a sign that the Lord *wanted* the people to be free. That's what those in the Civil Rights Movement believed – that segregation was not God's will, no matter how much white people told them it was, and that therefore to do nothing in that circumstance was to collude with evil and oppression. So they would organize and march and boycott and resist the evil of racism. African Americans have a long history of suffering, and the spirituals that had enabled them to 'keep on keeping on', as Martin Luther King described it, would accompany them once more on the long march to freedom.

The story of the Civil Rights Movement is an inspiring one. It achieved desegregation, civil rights, equality under the law. It also paid a high price in suffering. Its songs are converting ones. They converted me, they changed my life far more than any rally, altar call or Bible study ever did. Songs like this one:

> Oh freedom, oh freedom, oh freedom over me.
> And before I'd be a slave, I'd be buried in my grave
> And go home to my Lord and be free.
>
> (African-American spiritual)

I am not black. I am not an American. I did not suffer racism or segregation. But at the age of 13, I knew that this vision of Christianity, and this Jesus, articulated and embodied in the moral passion and costly commitment of Martin Luther King and his colleagues, and in people I knew personally as well, was something worth giving my life to. I have never changed my mind about that.

I learned these songs on Iona from people who shared that conviction. Some of them were Americans – black and white – involved in that struggle, who shared their stories with the Iona Community. Others were community members who had been working in Africa, and had been participating in the liberation movements of countries struggling to free themselves from European colonialism. They too had brought songs back to Scotland learned in the heat of economic, political and racial oppression somewhere else, and it was from that time in the 1960s that the explosion of words and music of the world church into the Iona Community began.

Vietnam War opposition

By the late 1960s, Martin Luther King had begun to speak out against the Vietnam War, encountering in the process even more hostility. The opposition to this long, morally compromised involvement, which brutalized so many, corrupted so many and failed to achieve any American objectives while staining its international reputation, became global, and its songs became global too. This movement also was non-violent, many Christians were part of it, and the biblical imagery was once again evident in the songs. For example, based on Isaiah 2.3–4, protesters sang:

> I'm gonna lay down my sword and shield, down by the riverside
> I ain't gonna study war no more.
>
> (African-American spiritual)

Demonstrations and marches took place across the world, and young people in particular mobilized, as part of a youth and student movement that challenged what they saw as a materialist, violent and compromised social order. In England, 100,000 people protested against the Vietnam War. In France, student protests against police brutality in May 1968 were joined by a strike of 10 million workers, and brought down the government. Later that year, a period of political liberalization in Czechoslovakia, known as the Prague Spring, was brutally put down when Soviet tanks occupied the country.

The pattern of peaceful demonstrations being met with state brutality came to a head in 1970, when four students, peacefully protesting the American invasion of Cambodia, were shot dead by the Ohio National Guard at Kent State University. The anti-war movement was swelled by millions of Americans who were calling into question a government that killed its own young in defence of its foreign policy. Eventually, the combination of military failure against a guerrilla army and hostile public opinion forced the United States to withdraw defeated from the devastated countries of South-East Asia. Bob Dylan's questioning anthem, 'How many roads must a man walk down?' seemed appropriate to a sombre mood.

The women's movement

By the 1970s, I had been on my first demonstration, against the Vietnam War, and was well on my way to becoming an activist.

By now, the focus of much of my activism had become the women's movement. I am a feminist, by which I mean someone who believes in the equal status and value of women, advocates for equal rights and responsibilities for women, and seeks measures that redress imbalances of well-being, health and education for women. Why am I a feminist? Let me put it this way. When I was a teenager:

- it was legal to pay women less than men for doing exactly the same job;
- it was legal to discriminate against women in employment, vocational training, education and the provision of goods and services;
- it was legal to exclude women from a wide range of premises and activities because they were women;
- it was legal for a woman to be forced to resign from her job if she got married;
- it was legal for a woman to have to obtain her husband's written consent to open a bank account or take out a mortgage;
- it was legal for a man to rape his wife;
- it was illegal for a woman to have an abortion for any reason whatsoever.

All of these things have changed, in Britain at least. I am proud to have been part of the movement that brought about these changes.

People often tell me that there is no need for feminism now. This fails to take account of the global pandemic that is violence against women; recognized as a major health hazard to women by the British Medical Association, but found in every country in the world. Violence against women takes many forms, as this book has already outlined. But there are other forms of violence of which women are disproportionately victims:

- 70 per cent of the world's 1200 million poor are women;
- 66 per cent of the world's illiterate people are women – in Asia and Africa, the figure reaches 70 per cent;
- 80 per cent of the world's refugees and uprooted peoples are women;
- the majority of people now testing HIV-positive are women.[1]

This is why I am still a feminist. And because I am a religious feminist, I have also learned to make a critique of the moral inferiority and practical inequality that much Christian theology and practice has imposed on women, and of the aspects of it which have legitimized violence against women.

In 1987, along with three members of the Women's Guild, I represented the Church of Scotland at the World Congress of Women in Moscow. It was during the days of perestroika, just before the end of the Cold War, and the thousands of women at the Congress from all over the world had the clear sense that something was changing. We received a warm welcome from Muscovites, and on the last night attended a ceremonial banquet in the Great Hall of Congress. After the dinner and speeches, the women got up and started to dance. They pulled flowers from the floral decorations and handed them to the dark-suited, armed security men who, trained to deal with violent incidents, had no idea how to respond to foreign women giving them roses. Then someone began to sing, and within a moment, five thousand women of every nationality, race, religion and background had linked arms and were singing that universal song of hope and freedom, 'We shall overcome some day'.

The peace movement

By the early 1980s, I had become a member of the Iona Community, attracted by its Rule of prayer and action for justice and peace, and particularly by its commitment to non-violence. At this time, I became increasingly involved in the peace movement's campaign against the global arms trade, and against nuclear weapons, which is a core commitment of the Iona Community. In 1981, 36 Welsh women, including a member of the Iona Community, set out from Cardiff to walk to the US airbase at Greenham Common 120 miles away. The group, called Women for Life on Earth, wanted to protest against the announcement that NATO cruise missiles were to be stored at the base. They captured the interest of the media by chaining themselves to the perimeter fence, demanding an open debate with the government on nuclear armament. This group became the Greenham Common Women's Peace Camp, where hundreds of women lived in tents and polythene shelters known as 'benders', and tens of thousands of other women came to join in non-violent demonstrations.

Greenham Common provided a model for non-violent direct action, still used by justice, peace and environmental activists across the world. It fostered an environment where women learned that they didn't need to speak or act on men's terms, that they could act independently in the service of life on earth. Above all, it was hugely influential in making people as a whole more aware of the issues surrounding nuclear weapons. At a time when nuclear proliferation and nuclear reduction treaties are under threat, and when our government is planning to upgrade Britain's Trident nuclear capability, regardless of the views of the British public, which are consistently opposed to this, it seems a good time to remember Greenham – and to remember its songs as well. The most famous of these was an affirmation of the spirit, and, also reflecting the times, the first time that female imagery made its way into the spiritual canon – it's amazing how many people still think that God is a man!

You can't kill the spirit, she is like a mountain
Old and strong, she goes on and on and on.[2]

The anti-apartheid movement

The peace movement was not the only place where resistance was going on in the face of apparently insuperable obstacles. On another continent, in South Africa, the liberation struggle against apartheid was at its most critical stage. By this time, I was living on Iona, and at Easter 1985, John Bell taught us a collection of songs entitled 'Freedom is coming', which came to us like water struck from the rock, bringing both inspiration and challenge. Collected by a Swede, Anders Nyberg, they came directly from the lived experience of suffering and hope of people for whom song was often the only form of resistance left open to them. These were the last years of apartheid rule, a white supremacist and racist system that denied the majority black population any democratic rights, classified people according to skin colour and criminalized interracial marriage; and the country, by now effectively a white police state, was more or less in a constant state of emergency. Massacres as a response to non-violent civil protest were routine. Draconian laws that forbade people to meet in groups of more than three, and brutal police repression, meant that worship and funerals, of which there were many of people who died by violence, were often the only ways that people could express their legitimate aspirations. Once again, the songs of faith of this 93 per cent Christian country became an articulation of a costly discipleship.

Across the world, people joined the anti-apartheid movement. In Britain, in spite of the fact that the Conservative government of Margaret Thatcher colluded with, and gave comfort to, the apartheid regime, hundreds of thousands marched, wrote letters, and boycotted South African goods in economic sanctions that played an important part in ending apartheid. The Iona Community had been deeply involved in this movement – some members had been banned, others deported or exiled from South Africa. So we sang these songs of freedom from South Africa. We sang them on Iona in solidarity with those who endured what we only heard about, on marches, and outside the South African Consulate in Glasgow. We sang them as part of a global movement for justice, knowing that the greatest burden was being borne by those facing bullets and whips in the townships of South Africa. We sang them, and what we discovered was that whatever political impact they might have in changing South Africa, the greatest impact was on us. They were changing us. These also were converting songs.

They confronted us with a Jesus who refused the military option and chose instead the way of loving non-violence and self-offering, who stood beside those who were oppressed, humiliated and excluded, who loved justice and gave hope. A Jesus who said that the day of the Lord was not a thousand years in the future, not in some pie in the sky when you die – a theological premise whose jacket is on a very shaky nail, and which mostly serves the interests of those who much prefer it if the poor and wretched of the earth can be persuaded to postpone salvation until they're dead – the day of the Lord is now, here, today. A Jesus who turned away from racism, and lived welcoming to all. A Jesus who was angry with those who fleeced the poor, especially when they did it in the name of religion. But a Jesus who also said we must love our enemies and overcome evil with good. The songs confronted us with a Jesus who said, there is another way, choose which way you will follow, who said, *freedom is coming, oh yes it is.*[3]

A spirituality for the long haul

There is another South African song we sing often on Iona: '*Hamba nathi khululu wethu*: Come with us for the journey is long'. All of the social movements I have described took many years of struggle to reach their goals (and in all of them, arrival did not mean giving up, it simply meant setting out again from their new destination). Some were on the front line of these movements, others played supporting and encouraging roles. But all of them had times of great weariness, disappointment, even despair. All of them had to face the challenge of what Martin Luther King described so eloquently as 'keeping on keeping on'.

For people committed to overcoming poverty and working for economic and environmental justice, this is equally a challenge. The Make Poverty History campaign of 2005 had almost unprecedented success in mobilizing people of goodwill across the world to seek three key goals: debt reduction and cancellation, trade justice and more and better aid. Some 250,000 people of all ages, descriptions, political and religious beliefs from NGOs, voluntary organizations, churches, trade unions, aid agencies and many who were marching for the first time, gathered in Edinburgh in an impressive display of support and solidarity for Making Poverty History. But progress, though there was undoubtedly some, has been slow since then, and for people used to more immediate solutions, intensely frustrating. A spirituality for the long haul is essential for people seeking justice.

Christians have deep wells to draw upon in 'keeping on keeping on'. I have spoken already about the importance of song. And among the most significant resources are the biblical ones, in particular those of the prophetic tradition, the great stories of the Hebrew Bible, and the Gospels. If we want to look at human behaviour, economics, relationship to land, in both their most destructive and most creative manifestations, this is a good place to look.

All people who are confronting radical change (and that really means all of us now) are somewhere on an Exodus journey. Perhaps we are comfortable at *home*, certainly not looking for change, happy to pull the blinds and blot out what is going on outside. But as we know, change is our only constant. Sometimes we try to resist engaging with change and deny the need to do so. There are plenty of biblical examples of people like that.

To begin to engage with change can sometimes seem like a kind of voluntary *exile*. Justice and peace activists in the church often find that. And sometimes, people find themselves in exile in a completely involuntary fashion. We are kicked out of our comfortable contentment! But even those who resist like anything find that change eventually affects us too. We too start to feel less at home, less comfortable and secure. The main characteristic of exile, whether it is brutal and oppressive, or anxious and disgruntled, or even principled and chosen, is that it looks back; its point of reference is the way things used to be in a place we used to belong. Its deepest experience is of loss. So a fundamental part of the exilic experience is bereavement. People in pastoral ministry learn about the stages of grief: shock, denial, anger, deep sadness. As justice campaigners, we have to allow our communities, and ourselves, to go through a grieving process, to mourn the land we have left. In a culture which is terrified of failure, loss and grief, finding the appropriate spaces for lamentation is not easy, and these things squeeze their way into very peculiar cracks sometimes, but I think it is essential. The biblical tradition of community lamentation is one important way in which people in huge crisis have responded and sought to find a way through their disempowerment. The book of Lamentations, sitting firmly in the middle of the prophetic books of the Hebrew Bible, laments the fall of Jerusalem and the beginning of the Babylonian captivity. Its poems are still used today in Jewish liturgy. It has allowed people to name their loss, their complicity and their fear, to turn passive despair into active mourning and to release the energy trapped in maintaining denial into energy for action and change. Lamentation has been an important aspect of all movements for justice, peace and freedom.

Eventually, if people are allowed to name and take leave of and lament what we have lost, there comes a time to move on. And that happens when people want to look forward rather than back, when, more than we want to mourn, we want to live!

It happens when we recognize that we have to tear up the maps that don't help us find a way any more. We're ready to move into uncharted territory, we're ready to go into the desert.

The main characteristic of the *desert*, the wilderness, for the people of Israel, was that it was featureless. There were no signposts, and the old maps were no use. They wandered around for years, in what is actually a very small area, lost, directionless and trying to work out what it meant to be a people. The vast screeds in the Pentateuch, the first five books of the Bible, laying down laws for this, that and the next thing, are really all about an uprooted people creating an identity for themselves. There was never enough to eat, the water was bad and they were constantly falling out among themselves. We know some of them wanted to go back to slavery in Egypt. We know they made somewhat of a detour to worship a golden bull they created for themselves. We know they were under attack from time to time, and that they were beset with many temptations, just as, millennia later, Jesus was in the desert. But through their long haul, I think they were trying to develop an ecological spirituality, a human ecology.

We too are in this for the long haul; transformation and creativity are more than just reacting to change. It will take years for the new to emerge fully, and, like Moses or Martin Luther King, we may not cross over into the Promised Land. But how we *live* the desert rather than just wandering it will shape what kind of land we find our way to.

So here are some questions that I have found it helpful in practising a spirituality for the long haul, both to ask myself, and to share with others.

Spiritual questions

God says: I will woo you,
and lead you into the wilderness
and speak to your heart.

(cf. Hosea 2.14)

1 Our community of justice and love

It is very hard to be a campaigner and activist on your own. We all need a community of accountability and support. It doesn't need to be a large community – perhaps it's a group of people in your church (if we are lucky, it may even be the whole congregation). Or it could be a prayer group, a women's or youth group, colleagues at work. If none of these seem likely, then we could volunteer to campaign with Christian Aid or any one of hundreds of organizations, and find people who share our concerns and will become our friends. So, the question is, 'Who are our community?'

2 Telling our story

The people of Israel had to keep telling their story; the one that got them through the times of exile, loss and wandering in the wilderness and that gave them hope for the future. Their story was, 'You will be a nation.' We have to keep telling our story. What is our story? What are the things that speak to our hearts of belonging and affirmation, of survival in times of loss and struggle, of finding new directions and hope for the future?

3 Lamentation

Where have we taken part in, or observed, lamentation, either religious or social? One example might be funerals, such as that of Princess Diana or world religious or political leaders. Others might be vigils, Ash Wednesday, the aftermath of disasters. What form does lamentation take for us? What do we lament the passing of?

4 The pillar of cloud and the pillar of fire

During the day, the LORD went in front of them in a pillar of cloud to show them the way, and during the night he went in front of them in a pillar of fire to give them light, so that they could travel night and day. The pillar of cloud

was always in front of the people during the day, and the
pillar of fire at night. (Exodus 13.21–22)

What are our pillar of cloud and our pillar of fire, as an individual and in our movement? What or who shows us the way?
What or who gives us light?

5 Manna and sweet water

When the dew evaporated, there was something thin and
flaky on the surface of the desert . . . Moses said, 'No one
is to keep any of it for tomorrow.' But some of them did
not listen to Moses and saved part of it. The next morning
it was full of worms and smelt rotten . . . every morning,
each one gathered as much as he needed, and when the
sun grew hot, what was left on the ground melted . . . The
people of Israel called the food manna . . . it tasted like
biscuits made of honey . . . The Israelites ate manna for
the next forty years . . . (Exodus 16.14ff.)

The people were very thirsty, and continued to complain
to Moses, 'Why did you bring us out of Egypt? To kill us
and our children and our livestock with thirst?' . . . The
LORD said to Moses . . . 'I will stand before you on a rock
at Mount Sinai. Strike the rock, and water will come out
of it for the people to drink.' (Exodus 17.3–7)

What sustains us and feeds us spiritually? What refreshes us?

6 Our temptations

Jesus was tempted in the desert. We too have temptations to
overcome. Some of these might include:

- harking back to captivity
- letting our fears and illusions run away with us
- making rules that are not appropriate to our context
- wanting to bypass the work
- wanting to live with certainty and have answers

- needing to see the outcomes
- thinking we have to fix things
- and that we know how to save everyone.

Perhaps God means others to save us! What are our temptations that we need to resist?

7 Our ministering angels

In the desert, angels came and ministered to Jesus. Who are the guardian angels of our movement? Who are the people who have been guardian angels to us?

Going on

Being in the desert on a long journey to a new land has many challenges. It is a testing-place. But it also has gifts. Sometimes it is easier to see the contours of the landscape, and the rock beneath the sand. We learn to travel more lightly. The miracle of survival and the grace of faith deepen tenacity and strengthen determination, and peace comes in going on. And our horizons inevitably widen. We live hopefully.

> The rejoicing of a private and exclusive community fails to invite all to hope. That is not the gospel. Hope with all creation and rejoice with all creation! What a far-reaching horizon! This horizon is not a hallucination. For God, no one is stranger. Every person – whatever his or her cultural, religious, racial, political, sexual identity – is known to God as an irreplaceable and incomparable person. This is the root of God's wholesome ecumenism. But when our actions say, 'I am not my brother's keeper' – the clearest, most understandable expression of sin – we treat God as a stranger. It is to look upon others as pollution. This destroys the foundation for hope in the world. To hope is to love your neighbour as yourself.[4]

Notes

Introduction: Born into complicity

1 Kosuke Koyama, from an address given at the Eighth WCC General Assembly, Harare, Zimbabwe, 1998.
2 Janet Morley, from *Celebrating Women*, ed. Hannah Ward, Jennifer Wild and Janet Morley (London: SPCK, 1995), p. 69. Reproduced by permission.

1 The spirituality of economics

1 From the WWF Living Planet Index (October 1998), and available at <www.wwf.org.uk/news/n_0000000307.asp>.
2 Quoted in Kathy Galloway, *A Scotland Where Everyone Matters: A Report on Church Action on Poverty's Scottish Poverty Indicators Project* (Church Action on Poverty 2002). Available through Church Action on Poverty's website at <www.church-poverty.org.uk>.
3 Galloway, *A Scotland Where Everyone Matters*.
4 From a speech given at the Memorial Service in Honour of the STS-107 Crew, Space Shuttle Columbia, 4 February 2003.
5 Archbishop Njongonkulu Ndungane, speaking at the 2002 AGM of the South African New Economics Network (SANE).
6 Ndungane, speaking at the 2002 AGM of SANE.

2 Sharing the blessing

1 G. A. Studdert Kennedy, 'Set your affections on things above' in *The Unutterable Beauty: The Collected Poetry of G. A. Studdert Kennedy* (London: Hodder & Stoughton, 1927).

3 *Bambalela*: Never give up

1 From 'A Guguletu Journal', written by Peter Millar, a member of the Iona Community (2005).
2 Millar, 'Guguletu Journal'.
3 Millar, 'Guguletu Journal'.

4 Monica Furlong, source unknown.
5 From Edwin Cameron, *Witness to AIDS* (Tafelberg 2005).
6 Millar, 'Guguletu Journal'.
7 Millar, 'Guguletu Journal'.

4 Living with difference

1 John L. Bell, 'Beside the streams of Babylon' from *Psalms of Patience, Protest and Praise* (Glasgow: Wild Goose Publications, 1993). Reproduced by permission.
2 Peter Cruchley-Jones, from 'Life in All its Fullness', Bible Studies on Ruth and Mary for the World Alliance of Reformed Churches, *Coracle* 4/21 (2006).
3 John L. Bell, 'I will give what I have' from *I Will Not Sing Alone* (Glasgow: Wild Goose Publications, 2004). Reproduced by permission.
4 Kosuke Koyama, from an address given at the Eighth WCC General Assembly, Harare, Zimbabwe, 1998.
5 Koyama, from an address given at the Eighth WCC General Assembly.
6 Robert Burns, 'To a Louse'.

5 The power of human dignity

1 Musimbi Kanyoro in *Your Story is My Story, Your Story is Our Story*, the book of the Decade Festival of Churches in Solidarity with Women (Geneva: WCC Publications, 1999).
2 From an address given by Kosuke Koyama at the Eighth WCC General Assembly, Harare, Zimbabwe, 1998.
3 'From You I Receive', © 1969 Nathan Segal, published in Unitarian Universalist Association, *Singing the Living Tradition* (Boston: Skinner House Books, 1993). Reproduced by permission.

6 Living hopefully

1 Calculated by Jubilee Debt Campaign and World Development Movement, using figures from Human Development Report 2006, Global Development Finance 2006 and Intergovernmental Panel on Climate Change 2007. Carbon emissions: 2003 figures. Debt: 2005 figures.
2 See Christian Aid's website section on 'Climate Change'.

3 From an address given by Kosuke Koyama at the Eighth WCC General Assembly, Harare, Zimbabwe, 1998.
4 Source unknown.

7 The journey is long

1 Figures from the UN Department of Public Information (2002), and available at <www.un.org/millenniumgoals/MDGs-FACT-SHEET1.pdf>.
2 'You Can't Kill the Spirit': © Naomi Littlebear Morena 1975.
3 From the song 'Freedom is Coming', South African traditional, Copyright © 1990 Wild Goose Publications, Iona Community, Glasgow, G2 3DH, Scotland. Reproduced by permission.
4 From an address given by Kosuke Koyama at the Eighth WCC General Assembly, Harare, Zimbabwe, 1998.

For further information and action

- To find out more about Christian Aid and the issues affecting global poverty (including climate change, trade justice, HIV/AIDS, emergencies, conflict) visit the Christian Aid website at <www.christianaid.org.uk> or write to Christian Aid, 35 Lower Marsh, London SE1 7RL. Tel. (+44) 020 7620 4444.
- To find out more about the United Nations Millennium Development Goals, visit: <www.un.org/millenniumgoals/index.html>.
- To find out more about poverty in Britain, and about the experience of asylum-seekers in Britain, contact Church Action on Poverty: <www.church-poverty.org.uk>, Church Action on Poverty, Central Buildings, Oldham Street, Manchester M1 1JQ. Tel. (+44) 0161 236 9321.
- To find out more about the Iona Community and the Camas Centre, visit <www.iona.org.uk>, The Iona Community, Savoy House, 140 Sauchiehall Street, Glasgow G2 3DH. Tel. (+44) 0141 332 6343.
- To find out more about songs of the world church, visit <ionabooks.com>, Wild Goose Publications, Savoy House, 140 Sauchiehall Street, Glasgow G2 3DH. Tel. (+44) 0141 332 6292.
- To find out more about the J. L. Zwane church and centre, Guguletu, visit <www.jlzwane.sun.ac.za>.